THE BEGINNER'S COOKBOOK

SIMPLE · EASY · DELICIOUS

pil

Publications International, Ltd.

Photograph on front cover (center top) and page 179 © Shutterstock.com.

Pictured on the front cover *(clockwise from top left):* Southwestern Sloppy Joes *(page 80),* Super Fudgy Brownies *(page 178),* Cauliflower, Sausage and Gouda Sheet Pan *(page 84),* Creamy Chicken Vegetable Soup *(page 30),* Pepperoni Pizza Bagels *(page 88)* and Spicy Chicken Rigatoni *(page 121).*

Pictured on the back cover *(clockwise from top left):* Sheet Pan Chicken and Sausage Supper *(page 41),* Baja Burritos *(page 112),* Crunchy Ice Cream Pie *(page 174)* and Smashed Potatoes *(page 139).*

ISBN: 978-1-63938-454-9

Manufactured in China.

8 7 6 5 4 3 2 1

Microwave Cooking: Microwave ovens vary in wattage. Use the cooking times as guidelines and check for doneness before adding more time.

WARNING: Food preparation, baking and cooking involve inherent dangers: misuse of electric products, sharp electric tools, boiling water, hot stoves, allergic reactions, foodborne illnesses and the like, pose numerous potential risks. Publications International, Ltd. (PIL) assumes no responsibility or liability for any damages you may experience as a result of following recipes, instructions, tips or advice in this publication.

While we hope this publication helps you find new ways to eat delicious foods, you may not always achieve the results desired due to variations in ingredients, cooking temperatures, typos, errors, omissions or individual cooking abilities.

Let's get social!

@Publications_International

@PublicationsInternational

www.pilbooks.com

CONTENTS

CRUSTLESS SPINACH QUICHE

[makes 6 servings]

8 eggs
1 cup half-and-half
1 teaspoon Italian seasoning
¾ teaspoon salt

½ teaspoon black pepper
1 package (10 ounces) frozen chopped spinach, thawed and squeezed dry
1¼ cups (5 ounces) shredded Italian cheese blend

1 Preheat oven to 350°F. Spray 8-inch round baking pan with nonstick cooking spray.

2 Beat eggs, half-and-half, Italian seasoning, salt and pepper in medium bowl with whisk or fork until well blended. Stir in spinach and cheese; mix well. Pour into prepared pan.

3 Bake 33 minutes or until toothpick inserted into center comes out clean. Remove pan to wire rack; cool 10 minutes before serving.

4 To remove quiche from pan, run knife around edge of pan to loosen. Invert quiche onto plate; invert again onto serving plate. Cut into wedges.

MEDITERRANEAN ARTICHOKE OMELET
[makes 1 serving]

2 eggs
1 tablespoon grated Parmesan cheese
2 tablespoons olive oil
3 canned artichoke bottoms,
    drained and diced (see Tip)

1 ounce (about 2 pieces) roasted
    red peppers, diced
½ teaspoon minced garlic
    Salsa (optional)

1 Beat eggs in small bowl with whisk or fork. Stir in cheese.

2 Heat oil in medium nonstick skillet over medium-high heat. Add artichokes; cook and stir 2 to 3 minutes or until beginning to brown. Add roasted peppers; cook and stir 2 minutes or until liquid has evaporated. Add garlic; cook and stir 30 seconds. Remove to small plate; cover with foil to keep warm.

3 Add egg mixture to skillet. Lift edge of omelet with spatula to allow any uncooked portion to flow underneath. Cook 1 to 2 minutes or until omelet is almost set.

4 Spoon artichoke mixture onto half of omelet; fold other half of omelet over filling with spatula. Cook 2 minutes or until set. Serve with salsa, if desired.

NOTE Raw eggs will turn green if combined with raw artichokes because of a chemical reaction between the two foods. Cooking the artichokes separately will prevent this from happening.

TIP The most commonly available canned artichoke product at most grocery stores is artichoke hearts; artichoke bottoms may be difficult to find. You can substitute 3 to 4 artichoke hearts, drained and chopped, for the bottoms; proceed with the recipe as directed.

FRUITY APPLE OATMEAL

[makes 4 to 6 servings]

3 cups old-fashioned oats, divided

½ cup finely diced pitted dates

½ cup finely diced dried apple

⅓ cup raisins

¼ cup packed dark brown sugar

½ teaspoon salt

½ teaspoon ground cinnamon

¹⁄₁₆ teaspoon ground nutmeg

2 cups water

2 cups milk, plus additional for serving

1 Combine oats, dates, apple, raisins, brown sugar, salt, cinnamon and nutmeg in medium bowl; mix well.

2 Bring water to a boil in large saucepan over high heat. Stir in oat mixture and 2 cups milk; mix well. Reduce heat to medium; cook 5 to 7 minutes or until oatmeal is thick and creamy, stirring frequently. Serve with additional milk, if desired.

> **TIP** You can customize this oatmeal recipe to suit your taste and to use the ingredients you have in your pantry. Substitute dried figs, apricots and/or cranberries for the dates, dried apple and raisins if you prefer. Dark brown sugar contains more molasses and has a slightly stronger flavor than light brown sugar; you can use either one. And you can swap out the regular milk for an alternative such as oat milk, rice milk or almond milk if you or your family is following a plant-based diet.

BREAKFAST BURRITOS
[makes 4 servings]

1 tablespoon butter
½ cup red or green bell pepper, chopped
2 green onions, sliced
6 eggs
2 tablespoons milk

½ teaspoon salt
4 (7-inch) flour tortillas, warmed
½ cup shredded Colby Jack or Mexican cheese blend
Salsa or pico de gallo

1 Melt butter in medium nonstick skillet over medium heat. Add bell pepper and green onions; cook and stir about 3 minutes or until vegetables are softened.

2 Beat eggs, milk and salt in medium bowl with whisk or fork until blended. Pour mixture into skillet. Reduce heat to low; cook about 4 minutes or until eggs are just set, stirring gently. (Eggs should be soft with no liquid remaining.)

3 Spoon one fourth of egg mixture down center of each tortilla; top with 2 tablespoons cheese. Roll up to enclose filling. Serve with salsa.

> **TIP** To warm tortillas, wrap them loosely in waxed paper or place them in a food storage bag and microwave at HIGH for 30 seconds. Or you can warm in the oven by wrapping them in foil and heating at 350°F for about 10 minutes.

BLUEBERRY PANCAKES
[makes 10 to 12 pancakes]

2 tablespoons plus 2 teaspoons butter
1¼ cups milk
1 egg, beaten
1¼ cups all-purpose flour
½ cup fresh blueberries

¼ cup packed brown sugar
1 tablespoon baking powder
½ teaspoon salt
Powdered sugar and maple syrup

1 Melt butter in large skillet over medium heat. Pour butter into medium bowl, leaving thin film of butter on skillet. Set skillet aside.

2 Add milk and egg to melted butter in bowl; beat with whisk or fork until well blended.

3 Combine flour, blueberries, brown sugar, baking powder and salt in large bowl; mix well, making sure brown sugar is broken up. Add milk mixture; stir just until blended. (Do not overmix or pancakes will be tough. There should be no visible flour streaks but the batter can be a little lumpy.)

4 Return skillet to stove over medium heat. Pour batter into skillet, ¼ cup at a time, leaving about 1 inch between pancakes. Cook about 3 minutes or until bottoms are golden brown and small bubbles are forming on top. Turn pancakes with spatula; cook 2 to 3 minutes or until golden brown. Dust with powdered sugar; serve with maple syrup.

FABULOUS FETA FRITTATA

[makes 4 servings]

8 **eggs**
¼ **cup chopped fresh basil**
¼ **cup whipping cream or half-and-half**
¼ **teaspoon salt**
¼ **teaspoon black pepper**

2 **tablespoons butter or olive oil**
1 **package (4 ounces) crumbled feta cheese with basil and sun-dried tomatoes**
¼ **cup pine nuts (optional)**

1 Preheat broiler.

2 Beat eggs, basil, cream, salt and pepper in medium bowl with whisk or fork until well blended. Melt butter in large ovenproof skillet over medium heat, tilting skillet to coat bottom and side.

3 Pour egg mixture into skillet. Cover and cook 8 to 10 minutes or until eggs are set around edge (center will be wet). Sprinkle with cheese and pine nuts, if desired.

4 Transfer skillet to broiler; broil 4 to 5 inches from heat source 2 minutes or until center is set. Cut into wedges.

TIP If your skillet is not ovenproof, wrap the handle in heavy-duty foil.

PERFECT FRENCH TOAST

[makes 4 servings]

Orange Butter (optional,
   recipe follows)
4 eggs
½ cup milk
2 tablespoons granulated sugar
1 teaspoon ground cinnamon

1 teaspoon vanilla
¼ teaspoon ground nutmeg
8 ounces French bread, cut
   diagonally into 8 slices
1 to 2 tablespoons butter
Powdered sugar (optional)

1 Prepare Orange Butter, if desired.

2 Beat eggs, milk, granulated sugar, cinnamon, vanilla and nutmeg in shallow bowl or baking dish with whisk or fork until well blended. Make sure egg yolks and whites are completely broken up and sugar is dissolved. Dip bread slices in egg mixture, turning to coat.

3 Heat 1 tablespoon butter in large skillet over medium heat. Add bread in single layer, leaving a little space between slices. (You'll need to cook the bread in two batches). Cook 3 minutes or until golden brown on bottom; turn and cook 3 minutes or until second side is golden brown. Repeat with remaining bread slices, adding additional butter if skillet is dry.

4 Sprinkle with powdered sugar, if desired. Serve with Orange Butter.

ORANGE BUTTER Place ⅓ cup whipped butter in small microwavable bowl; microwave on HIGH 10 seconds to soften. Stir in 2 tablespoons orange marmalade and 2 teaspoons honey until well blended.

ZUCCHINI OMELET WITH DILL

[makes 2 servings]

5 eggs

2 tablespoons milk

½ teaspoon dried dill weed

¼ plus ⅛ teaspoon salt, divided

⅛ teaspoon black pepper

1 tablespoon butter

1 cup diced zucchini

1 Beat eggs, milk, dill weed, ¼ teaspoon salt and pepper in medium bowl with whisk or fork until blended.

2 Melt butter in medium nonstick skillet over medium-high heat. Add zucchini and remaining ⅛ teaspoon salt; cook 4 minutes or until lightly browned, stirring occasionally.

3 Add egg mixture to skillet; cook until edges are set. Push edges toward center with spatula; tilt skillet to allow uncooked portion to flow underneath. When eggs are set, fold omelet over with spatula. Slide omelet onto plate; cut in half.

> **TIP** When you crack eggs for a recipe, it's best to do it against a flat surface like a countertop rather than the edge of a bowl—the flat surface will provide a cleaner break and you're less likely to end up with bits of eggshell in your mixing bowl.

PICANTE BLACK BEAN SOUP

[makes 6 to 8 servings]

4 slices bacon, cut into ½-inch pieces
1 large onion, chopped
1 clove garlic, minced
2 cans (about 15 ounces each) black beans, undrained
1 can (about 14 ounces) vegetable broth

1¼ cups water
¾ cup picante sauce, plus additional for serving
½ teaspoon salt
½ teaspoon dried oregano
¼ to ½ cup sour cream

1 Cook bacon in large saucepan over medium-high heat until crisp, stirring frequently. Drain on paper towel-lined plate.

2 Add onion and garlic to drippings in saucepan; cook and stir 3 minutes. Stir in beans with liquid, broth, water, ¾ cup picante sauce, ½ teaspoon salt and oregano; bring to a boil. Reduce heat to low; cover and simmer 20 minutes. Taste and add additional salt, if desired.

3 Top each serving with sour cream; sprinkle with bacon. Serve with additional picante sauce.

PESTO TORTELLINI SOUP

[makes 6 servings]

1 package (9 ounces) refrigerated cheese tortellini

3 cans (about 14 ounces each) chicken or vegetable broth

1 jar (7 ounces) roasted red peppers, drained and thinly sliced

¾ cup frozen green peas

3 to 4 cups packed stemmed fresh spinach

1 to 2 tablespoons pesto sauce

Grated Parmesan cheese (optional)

1 Cook tortellini according to package directions; drain.

2 Meanwhile, bring broth to a boil in large saucepan or Dutch oven over high heat. Add cooked tortellini, roasted peppers and peas; return to a boil. Reduce heat to medium; simmer 2 minutes.

3 Remove from heat; stir in spinach and pesto. Serve with cheese, if desired.

TIP To easily remove stems from spinach leaves, fold each leaf in half, then pull the stem toward the top of the leaf. Discard the stems.

SWEET POTATO AND HAM SOUP
[makes 6 servings]

1 tablespoon butter
1 leek, thinly sliced
1 clove garlic, minced
4 cups chicken broth
2 sweet potatoes, peeled and
    cut into ¾-inch pieces

8 ounces ham, cut into ½-inch pieces
½ teaspoon dried thyme
2 ounces stemmed fresh spinach,
    coarsely chopped

1 Melt butter in large saucepan over medium heat. Add leek and garlic; cook and stir about 3 minutes or until tender.

2 Add broth, sweet potatoes, ham and thyme; bring to a boil over high heat. Reduce heat to low; simmer 10 minutes or until sweet potatoes are tender.

3 Stir in spinach; cook 2 minutes or until spinach is wilted. Serve immediately.

TIP Leeks look like giant green onions; they are part of the allium family but they have a milder and sweeter flavor than onions. Before slicing them, cut of the dark green tops (which are very tough) so you're left with the white and light green parts. If the outer layer is bruised or slimy, peel that off, then cut the leeks in half lengthwise. You'll see many layers inside; these should be rinsed very well under cool water, as leeks often have a lot of dirt and sand inside. You can also slice the leeks before cleaning them. Place the leek slices in a colander and rinse well, stirring them around with your hand to make sure all the dirt and sand are gone.

GREEK LEMON AND RICE SOUP
[makes 6 to 8 servings]

2 tablespoons butter
⅓ cup minced green onions (see Tip)
6 cups chicken broth
⅔ cup uncooked long grain rice
4 eggs

Juice of 1 lemon
⅛ teaspoon black pepper
Fresh mint and lemon peel (optional)

1 Melt butter in medium saucepan over medium heat. Add green onions; cook and stir about 3 minutes or until tender.

2 Stir in broth and rice; bring to a boil over medium-high heat. Reduce heat to low; cover and simmer 20 to 25 minutes or until rice is tender.

3 Beat eggs in medium bowl. Stir in lemon juice and ½ cup hot broth mixture from saucepan until blended. (Adding a small amount of hot liquid to the eggs heats them gradually and prevents them from cooking or scrambling when you add them to the hot soup.)

4 Slowly pour egg mixture back into broth mixture in saucepan, stirring constantly. Cook and stir over low heat 2 to 3 minutes or until soup thickens enough to lightly coat spoon. *Do not boil.* Stir in pepper. Garnish with mint and lemon peel.

> **TIP** Mincing means cutting food into very small pieces (about ⅛ or 1⁄16 inch), which is usually done with a chef's knife. Minced vegetables are cut smaller than chopped or finely chopped vegetables; these tiny pieces are more easily incorporated into a dish, and when sautéed, they often melt into a dish, adding flavor without a noticeable texture.

STIR-FRY BEEF AND VEGETABLE SOUP

[makes 6 servings]

1 boneless beef top sirloin or top
round steak (about 1 pound)

2 teaspoons dark sesame oil, divided

3 cans (about 14 ounces each)
beef broth

1 package (16 ounces) frozen
stir-fry vegetables

3 green onions, thinly sliced

¼ cup stir-fry sauce

1 Cut beef in half lengthwise, then crosswise into ⅛-inch-thick strips.

2 Heat 1 teaspoon oil in large saucepan or Dutch oven over medium-high heat; tilt
pan to coat bottom with oil. Add half of beef in single layer. Cook 1 minute, without
stirring, until lightly browned on bottom. Turn and cook about 1 minute or until other
side is browned. Remove to plate. Repeat with remaining 1 teaspoon oil and beef.

3 Add broth to saucepan; bring to a boil over high heat, scraping up browned bits
from bottom of saucepan. Add stir-fry vegetables; cook over medium heat 3 to
5 minutes or until vegetables are heated through. Add beef, green onions and
stir-fry sauce; cook 1 minute.

> **TIP** When you're shopping for sesame oil—usually found in the Asian
> section of the supermarket—you may see both light and dark sesame oils on
> the shelf. Both are extracted from sesame seeds, but the light one is raw,
> untoasted sesame oil and is generally used for high heat cooking similar to
> vegetable, canola or other neutral oils. Dark sesame oil, also called toasted
> sesame oil, has a rich, strong, nutty flavor. It is sometimes used for quick
> cooking, but is more often added at the end of cooking or used in sauces
> and dressings where the heat doesn't diminish its flavor.

CREAMY CHICKEN VEGETABLE SOUP

[makes 4 servings]

2 cans (about 14 ounces each) chicken broth

12 ounces boneless skinless chicken thighs

1 clove garlic, minced

½ teaspoon dried thyme

½ (16-ounce) package frozen stir-fry vegetables

2 ounces uncooked egg noodles

1 zucchini, cut in half lengthwise and cut crosswise into ¼-inch slices

1 cup frozen corn, thawed

½ cup frozen peas

1 teaspoon salt

½ teaspoon black pepper

1 cup half-and-half

2 tablespoons finely chopped fresh parsley

1 Combine broth, chicken, garlic and thyme in large saucepan or Dutch oven; bring to a boil over medium-high heat. Reduce heat to low; cover and simmer 30 minutes or until chicken is very tender. Remove chicken to plate; set aside until cool enough to handle.

2 Meanwhile, add stir-fry vegetables, noodles, zucchini, corn, peas, salt and pepper to broth in saucepan; bring to a boil over medium-high heat. Reduce heat to medium; cook, uncovered, about 7 minutes or until noodles are almost tender.

3 Shred chicken into bite-size pieces. Add to saucepan with half-and-half and parsley; cook and stir 3 minutes or until heated through.

PASTA E FAGIOLI

[makes 8 servings]

2 tablespoons olive oil

1 cup chopped onion

3 cloves garlic, minced

2 cans (about 14 ounces each) Italian-style stewed tomatoes, undrained

3 cups vegetable broth

1 can (about 15 ounces) cannellini beans (white kidney beans),* undrained

¼ cup chopped fresh Italian parsley

1 teaspoon dried basil

¼ teaspoon black pepper

4 ounces uncooked small shell pasta

If cannellini beans are unavailable, substitute Great Northern beans.

1 Heat oil in large saucepan or Dutch oven over medium heat. Add onion and garlic; cook and stir 5 minutes or until onion is tender.

2 Add tomatoes, broth, beans with liquid, parsley, basil and pepper; bring to a boil over high heat, stirring occasionally. Reduce heat to low; cover and simmer 10 minutes.

3 Stir in pasta; cover and cook over medium heat 10 minutes or just until pasta is tender. Serve immediately.

NOTE Canned beans contain a thick liquid that is starchy and often high in sodium. Most recipes call for beans to be drained and rinsed before cooking, but sometimes the bean liquid is used as a thickener and may be added to soups and stews along with the beans.

HOT AND SOUR SOUP
[makes 4 servings]

2 cans (about 14 ounces each)
chicken broth
1 can (4 ounces) sliced mushrooms
2 tablespoons rice vinegar or white
wine vinegar
¼ to ½ teaspoon hot pepper sauce
2 tablespoons soy sauce

2 tablespoons cornstarch
1 egg, lightly beaten
2 green onions, thinly sliced,
plus additional for garnish
Thinly sliced red chile pepper
(optional)

1 Combine broth, mushrooms, vinegar and hot pepper sauce in large saucepan; bring to a boil over high heat.

2 Stir soy sauce into cornstarch in small bowl until smooth. Add to saucepan; cook and stir over medium-high heat until soup is slightly thickened.

3 Slowly pour in egg, stirring constantly in one direction 1 minute or until egg is cooked. Remove from heat; stir in two green onions. Garnish with additional green onion and chile pepper.

> **TIP** When a recipe uses cornstarch as a thickener, it's best to put the cornstarch in a bowl and then gradually stir in the liquid. If you reverse the order and add the cornstarch to a bowl of liquid, it can be difficult to get a smooth mixture without any lumps.

QUICK AND EASY RAVIOLI SOUP

[makes 8 servings]

8 ounces mild Italian sausage,
   casings removed
½ cup chopped onion
1 clove garlic, minced
2 cans (about 14 ounces each)
   chicken broth
2 cups water
1 package (9 ounces) frozen mini
   cheese-filled ravioli

1 can (about 15 ounces) chickpeas,
   rinsed and drained
1 can (about 14 ounces) diced
   tomatoes with mild green chiles
¾ teaspoon dried oregano
½ teaspoon black pepper
1 cup baby spinach
   Grated Parmesan cheese

1 Cook sausage, onion and garlic in large saucepan or Dutch oven over medium heat
   5 minutes or until sausage is cooked through, stirring to break up meat. Drain fat.
   Remove to medium bowl.

2 Add broth and water to saucepan; bring to a boil over medium-high heat. Add
   ravioli; cook 4 to 5 minutes or until tender.

3 Return sausage mixture to saucepan with chickpeas, tomatoes, oregano and
   pepper; cook about 5 minutes until heated through. Stir in spinach; cook
   1 minute or until wilted. Sprinkle with cheese.

SPICY THAI COCONUT SOUP
[makes 4 servings]

2 cups chicken broth

1 can (about 13 ounces) light coconut milk

1 tablespoon minced fresh ginger

½ to 1 teaspoon red curry paste

3 cups coarsely shredded cooked chicken

1 can (15 ounces) straw mushrooms, drained

1 can (about 8 ounces) baby corn, drained

2 tablespoons lime juice

¼ cup chopped fresh cilantro

1 Combine broth, coconut milk, ginger and curry paste in large saucepan; mix well. Add chicken, mushrooms and corn; bring to a simmer over medium heat. Cook 5 minutes or until heated through, stirring occasionally.

2 Stir in lime juice. Sprinkle with cilantro just before serving.

NOTE Red curry paste can be found in jars in the Asian food section of large grocery stores. Spice levels can vary between brands—start with ½ teaspoon, then add more as desired.

TIP A rotisserie chicken from the supermarket will yield 3 to 4 cups of shredded meat, or you can use leftover chicken or turkey for the recipe.

CHICKEN

SHEET PAN CHICKEN AND SAUSAGE SUPPER

[makes about 6 servings]

⅓ cup olive oil
2 tablespoons balsamic vinegar
1 teaspoon salt
1 teaspoon garlic powder
½ teaspoon black pepper
¼ teaspoon red pepper flakes
3 pounds bone-in chicken thighs and drumsticks

1 pound uncooked sweet Italian sausage (4 to 5 links), cut diagonally into 2-inch pieces
6 to 8 small red onions (about 1½ pounds), each cut into 6 wedges
3½ cups broccoli florets

1 Preheat oven to 425°F. Line baking sheet with foil, if desired.

2 Whisk oil, vinegar, salt, garlic powder, black pepper and red pepper flakes in small bowl until well blended. Combine chicken, sausage and onions on prepared baking sheet. Drizzle with oil mixture; toss until all ingredients are well coated. Spread meat and onions in single layer (chicken thighs should be skin side up).

3 Bake 30 minutes. Add broccoli to baking sheet; stir to coat broccoli with pan juices and turn sausage.

4 Bake 30 minutes or until broccoli is beginning to brown and chicken is cooked through (165°F).

PULLED CHICKEN SANDWICHES

[makes 4 servings]

1 cup water
1 cup barbecue sauce, divided
2 tablespoons Worcestershire sauce
2 pounds boneless skinless chicken
    thighs

1 small red onion, cut in half and
    thinly sliced
4 pretzel rolls or sandwich buns, split
½ cup cabbage slaw

1 Combine water, ¾ cup barbecue sauce and Worcestershire sauce in large saucepan; mix well. Add chicken and onion; stir to blend. (Liquid should just cover chicken; add additional water if necessary.) Bring to a simmer over medium-high heat.

2 Reduce heat to medium-low; cover and cook 35 minutes. Remove chicken to medium bowl; let stand 10 to 15 minutes or until cool enough to handle. Meanwhile, cook liquid in saucepan over medium-high heat 10 to 15 minutes or until reduced by half.

3 Shred chicken into bite-size pieces in bowl. (Use your hands or two forks to pull chicken apart.) Add remaining ¼ cup barbecue sauce and ¼ cup reduced cooking liquid; toss to coat. Serve remaining cooking liquid for dipping, if desired.

4 Serve chicken mixture on rolls with cabbage slaw.

CHICKEN PICCATA
[makes 4 servings]

3 tablespoons all-purpose flour
½ teaspoon salt
¼ teaspoon black pepper
4 boneless skinless chicken breasts
   (4 to 6 ounces each)
1 tablespoon olive oil
1 tablespoon butter

2 cloves garlic, minced
¾ cup chicken broth
1 tablespoon lemon juice
2 tablespoons chopped fresh
   Italian parsley
1 tablespoon capers, drained

1 Combine flour, salt and pepper in shallow dish; mix well. Reserve 1 tablespoon flour mixture for sauce.

2 Coat chicken with remaining flour mixture, shaking off excess.

3 Heat oil and butter in large skillet over medium heat. Add chicken; cook 4 to 5 minutes per side or until no longer pink in center. Transfer to serving platter; tent with foil to keep warm.

4 Add garlic to skillet; cook and stir over medium heat 1 minute. Add reserved flour mixture; cook and stir 1 minute. Add broth and lemon juice; cook and stir 2 minutes or until sauce thickens. Stir in parsley and capers; spoon sauce over chicken.

SIMPLE ROASTED CHICKEN
[makes 4 servings]

1 whole chicken (about 4 pounds)
3 tablespoons butter, softened
1½ teaspoons salt
1 teaspoon onion powder
1 teaspoon dried thyme

½ teaspoon garlic powder
½ teaspoon paprika
½ teaspoon black pepper
Fresh parsley sprigs and lemon
    wedges (optional)

1 Preheat oven to 425°F. Pat chicken dry; place in small baking dish or on baking sheet.

2 Combine butter, salt, onion powder, thyme, garlic powder, paprika and pepper in small microwavable bowl; mash with fork until well blended. Loosen skin on breasts and thighs; spread about one third of butter mixture under skin.

3 Microwave remaining butter mixture until melted. Brush melted butter mixture all over outside of chicken and inside cavity. Tie drumsticks together with kitchen string and tuck wing tips under.

4 Roast 20 minutes. *Reduce oven temperature to 375°F.* Roast 45 to 55 minutes or until chicken is cooked through (165°F), basting once with pan juices during last 10 minutes of cooking time. (Test the doneness by inserting an instant-read thermometer into the thickest part of the thigh.) Transfer chicken to cutting board; tent with foil to keep warm. Let stand 15 minutes before carving. Garnish with parsley and lemon wedges.

SESAME CHICKEN

[makes 4 servings]

1 pound boneless skinless chicken
   breasts or thighs, cut into
   1-inch pieces

⅔ cup teriyaki sauce, divided

2 teaspoons cornstarch

1 tablespoon peanut or vegetable oil

2 cloves garlic, minced

2 green onions, cut into ½-inch slices

1 tablespoon sesame seeds, toasted
   (see Tip)

1 teaspoon dark sesame oil

1 Combine chicken and ⅓ cup teriyaki sauce in medium bowl; toss to coat. Marinate in refrigerator 15 to 20 minutes.

2 Drain chicken; discard marinade. Stir remaining ⅓ cup teriyaki sauce into cornstarch in small bowl until smooth.

3 Heat peanut oil in large skillet over medium-high heat. Add chicken and garlic; cook and stir 3 minutes or until chicken is cooked through.

4 Stir cornstarch mixture; add to skillet. Cook and stir 1 minute or until sauce boils and thickens. Stir in green onions, sesame seeds and sesame oil.

> **TIP** To toast sesame seeds, cook them in a small skillet over medium-low heat about 3 minutes or until the seeds begin to pop and turn golden brown.

BALSAMIC CHICKEN

[makes 6 servings]

1½ teaspoons fresh rosemary leaves, minced, or ½ teaspoon dried rosemary

2 cloves garlic, minced

¾ teaspoon black pepper

½ teaspoon salt

6 boneless skinless chicken breasts (4 to 6 ounces each)

1 tablespoon olive oil

¼ cup balsamic vinegar

1 Combine rosemary, garlic, pepper and salt in small bowl; mix well. Place chicken in large bowl or baking dish; drizzle with oil and rub with spice mixture. Cover and refrigerate several hours.

2 Preheat oven to 450°F. Spray baking sheet or shallow roasting pan with nonstick cooking spray.

3 Place chicken on baking sheet; bake 10 minutes. Turn chicken and stir in 3 to 4 tablespoons water if drippings begin to stick to pan. Bake about 10 minutes or until chicken is golden brown and no longer pink in center. If pan is dry, stir in 1 to 2 tablespoons water to loosen drippings.

4 Drizzle vinegar over chicken on baking sheet. Transfer chicken to serving plates. Stir liquid left on baking sheet; drizzle over chicken.

TIP Fresh herbs add vibrant flavors to a dish, but sometimes they can be inconvenient—you may not want to stop at the grocery store for just one ingredient if you have the rest on hand, or you might not want to purchase a full package of fresh herbs when you only need a very small amount. The general rule of thumb when substituting dry herbs for fresh is to use a three-to-one ratio: If a recipe calls for 1 tablespoon of a chopped fresh herb, use 1 teaspoon of the dried herb instead.

SPICE-CRUSTED CHICKEN THIGHS

[makes 4 servings]

1 teaspoon garlic powder
1 teaspoon onion powder
1 teaspoon dried oregano
1 teaspoon ground thyme

1 teaspoon paprika
1 teaspoon salt
1 teaspoon black pepper
8 bone-in, skin-on chicken thighs

1 Preheat oven to 425°F. Spray baking sheet or shallow roasting pan with nonstick cooking spray or line with foil.

2 Combine garlic powder, onion powder, oregano, thyme, paprika, salt and pepper in small bowl; mix well.

3 Place chicken in large resealable food storage bag. Add spice mixture; seal bag and shake well to coat. Place chicken in single layer on baking sheet.

4 Roast 35 to 40 minutes or until chicken is browned and cooked through (165°F).

TIP You can substitute boneless, skinless chicken thighs for the bone-in, skin-on ones; they will take less time to cook (20 to 25 minutes). Always check the temperature with an instant-read thermometer; the timing can vary considerably depending on the size and thickness of your chicken thighs.

CHICKEN PESTO PIZZA

[makes 6 servings]

8 ounces chicken tenders
1 tablespoon olive oil
1 medium onion, thinly sliced
⅓ cup pesto sauce
3 medium plum tomatoes,
    thinly sliced

1 (12- to 14-inch) prepared pizza crust
1 cup (4 ounces) shredded mozzarella
    cheese

1 Preheat oven to 450°F. Cut chicken tenders into bite-size pieces.

2 Heat oil in large skillet over medium heat. Add chicken; cook and stir 2 minutes. Add onion and pesto; cook and stir about 3 minutes or until chicken is cooked through.

3 Arrange tomato slices and chicken mixture over pizza crust to within 1 inch of edge. Sprinkle with cheese.

4 Bake 8 minutes or until pizza is hot and cheese is melted and beginning to brown.

> **TIP** Chicken tenders (also called chicken breast tenders) are the strips of meat that are attached to the underside of a chicken breast, usually about 1½ inches wide and 5 inches long. Many supermarkets sell chicken tenders separately, or they may be sold attached to the chicken breast. If you can't find a package of chicken tenders for this recipe, you can purchase the same weight of boneless skinless chicken breasts and cut them lengthwise into strips about ½ inch thick.

OVEN BARBECUE CHICKEN
[makes 4 to 6 servings]

1 cup barbecue sauce
¼ cup honey
2 tablespoons soy sauce
2 teaspoons grated fresh ginger

½ teaspoon dry mustard
1 cut-up whole chicken
   (3 to 4 pounds)

1 Preheat oven to 350°F. Spray 13×9-inch baking dish or shallow roasting pan with nonstick cooking spray.

2 Combine barbecue sauce, honey, soy sauce, ginger and mustard in small bowl; mix well.

3 Place chicken skin side up in prepared baking dish; brush evenly with sauce mixture.

4 Bake 45 minutes or until chicken is cooked through (165°F), brushing occasionally with sauce.

TIP Fresh ginger is a knobby, bumpy-looking beige colored root available year round in the produce section. It has a thin, tough skin that should be peeled away—you can do this with a paring knife or by scraping a metal spoon against the ginger. Then use a box grater or microplane grater to grate the ginger; you'll need ½ to 1 inch of fresh ginger to get 2 teaspoons of grated ginger. (Only peel the amount you need.)

CHICKEN AND VEGGIE FAJITAS

[makes 6 servings]

1 pound boneless skinless chicken
    thighs, cut crosswise into strips
1 teaspoon dried oregano
1 teaspoon chili powder
½ teaspoon garlic salt
½ teaspoon ground cumin
1 tablespoon vegetable oil
2 bell peppers (preferably 1 red and
    1 green), cut into thin strips

4 thin slices large sweet or yellow
    onion, separated into rings
½ cup salsa
6 (8-inch) flour tortillas, warmed
½ cup chopped fresh cilantro
    or green onions
Sour cream (optional)

1 Combine chicken, oregano, chili powder, garlic salt and cumin in medium bowl; toss to coat.

2 Heat oil in large skillet over medium-high heat. Add chicken; cook and stir 5 to 6 minutes or until cooked through. Remove to plate.

3 Add bell peppers and onion to skillet; cook and stir 2 minutes over medium heat. Add salsa; cover and cook 6 to 8 minutes or until vegetables are tender. Uncover; return chicken and any accumulated juices to skillet. Cook and stir 2 minutes or until heated through.

4 Serve chicken mixture with tortillas; top with cilantro and sour cream, if desired.

SHEET PAN MEDITERRANEAN CHICKEN

[makes 6 servings]

¼ cup extra virgin olive oil

4 cloves garlic, thinly sliced

1 tablespoon red wine vinegar

2 teaspoons salt

1½ teaspoons smoked paprika

1 teaspoon dried oregano

½ teaspoon black pepper

6 boneless skinless chicken thighs
    (about 2 pounds)

2 cans (about 15 ounces each)
    chickpeas, rinsed and drained

3 pints grape tomatoes

½ cup pitted Kalamata olives,
    cut into halves

¾ cup crumbled feta cheese

½ cup chopped fresh Italian parsley

1 Preheat oven to 425°F. Line baking sheet with foil or spray with nonstick cooking spray.

2 Whisk oil, garlic, vinegar, salt, smoked paprika, oregano and pepper in large bowl until well blended. Add chicken, chickpeas, tomatoes and olives; stir to coat well. Spread mixture on prepared baking sheet. (Baking sheet will be very full.)

3 Bake 18 to 20 minutes or until chicken is cooked through (165°F) and tomatoes are beginning to burst. *Turn oven to broil;* broil 2 to 3 minutes or until chicken begins to brown.

4 Sprinkle with cheese and parsley. Serve with crusty bread, hot cooked orzo or rice, if desired.

MONGOLIAN BEEF

[makes 4 servings]

1¼ pounds beef flank steak
¼ cup cornstarch
3 tablespoons vegetable oil, divided
3 cloves garlic, minced
2 teaspoons grated fresh ginger
½ cup water

½ cup soy sauce
⅓ cup packed dark brown sugar
   Pinch red pepper flakes
2 green onions, diagonally sliced
   into 1-inch pieces
   Hot cooked rice (optional)

1 Cut flank steak in half lengthwise, then cut crosswise (against the grain) into ¼-inch slices. Combine beef and cornstarch in medium bowl; toss to coat.

2 Heat 1 tablespoon oil in large skillet over high heat. Add half of beef in single layer (do not crowd); cook 1 to 2 minutes per side or until browned. Remove to clean bowl. Repeat with remaining beef and 1 tablespoon oil.

3 Heat remaining 1 tablespoon oil in same skillet over medium heat. Add garlic and ginger; cook and stir 30 seconds. Add water, soy sauce, brown sugar and red pepper flakes; bring to a boil, stirring until well blended. Cook 8 minutes or until sauce is slightly thickened, stirring occasionally.

4 Return beef to skillet; cook 2 to 3 minutes or until sauce thickens and beef is heated through. Stir in green onions. Serve with rice, if desired.

SPAGHETTI AND MEATBALLS
[makes 4 servings]

12 ounces ground beef
4 ounces hot Italian sausage,
    casings removed
1 egg
2 tablespoons plain dry bread crumbs
1 teaspoon dried oregano

½ teaspoon salt
2 cups tomato-basil pasta sauce
8 ounces uncooked spaghetti
    Grated Parmesan cheese
    Chopped fresh basil (optional)

1 Preheat oven to 450°F. Spray baking sheet with nonstick cooking spray.

2 Combine beef, sausage, egg, bread crumbs, oregano and salt in medium bowl; mix gently. Shape mixture into 16 (1½-inch) meatballs. Place on prepared baking sheet; spray with cooking spray. Bake 12 minutes, turning once.

3 Pour pasta sauce into large skillet. Add meatballs; cook over medium heat 9 minutes or until sauce is heated through and meatballs are cooked through (160°F), stirring occasionally.

4 Meanwhile, cook spaghetti according to package directions. Drain spaghetti; top with meatballs and sauce. Sprinkle with cheese and basil, if desired.

BALSAMIC-GLAZED SIRLOIN AND SPINACH

[makes 4 servings]

5 tablespoons olive oil, divided

2 Vidalia or other sweet onions, thinly sliced

3 tablespoons balsamic vinegar, divided

1 teaspoon salt, divided

1 teaspoon coarsely ground black pepper

1 pound top sirloin steak (about 1 inch thick)

1 package (about 10 ounces) fresh spinach, stemmed and coarsely chopped

1 Heat 2 tablespoons oil in large skillet over medium-high heat. Add onions; cook 10 minutes or until softened, stirring occasionally. Sprinkle with 1 tablespoon vinegar and ½ teaspoon salt; cook 10 minutes or until beginning to brown. Remove to medium bowl; cover to keep warm.

2 Meanwhile, press pepper onto both sides of steak. Rub with ½ teaspoon vinegar; sprinkle with ¼ teaspoon salt.

3 Heat 1 tablespoon oil in same skillet over medium-high heat. Add steak; cook 5 minutes. Turn and cook 3 to 5 minutes for medium rare (135°F) or to desired doneness. Transfer steak to cutting board; tent with foil to keep warm. Let stand 5 minutes before slicing.

4 Add remaining 2 tablespoon oil to skillet. Add spinach; cover and cook 2 minutes. (Spinach will shrink down to fit in pan.) Stir spinach; cook 1 minute if necessary to wilt all of spinach. Stir in remaining vinegar and ¼ teaspoon salt; cook and stir 1 minute.

5 Cut steak into thin slices; serve over spinach and onions.

QUICK GREEK PITAS

[makes 6 servings]

1 pound ground beef

1 package (10 ounces) frozen chopped
   spinach, thawed and well drained

4 green onions, chopped

1 can (2¼ ounces) sliced black olives,
   drained

1 teaspoon dried oregano, divided

¼ teaspoon black pepper

1 large tomato, diced

1 cup plain yogurt

½ cup mayonnaise

6 (6-inch) pita bread rounds, warmed
   Lettuce leaves

1 cup (4 ounces) crumbled feta
   cheese

1 Cook beef in large skillet over medium-high heat 6 to 8 minutes or until browned, stirring to break up meat. Drain fat.

2 Add spinach, green onions, olives, ½ teaspoon oregano and pepper to skillet; cook and stir 2 minutes. Stir in tomato.

3 Combine yogurt, mayonnaise and remaining ½ teaspoon oregano in small bowl; mix well. Cut pita breads in half; line with lettuce leaves.

4 Stir cheese into beef mixture. Divide evenly among pita pockets; serve with yogurt sauce.

BEEF, MUSHROOM AND ONION SKILLET

[makes 4 servings]

2 tablespoons olive oil, divided
2 large sweet onions, sliced
¾ teaspoon salt, divided
4 teaspoons balsamic vinegar, divided
4 ounces mushrooms, sliced

1 boneless beef top sirloin
   (about 1 pound), cut
   into ½-inch-thick slices
¼ teaspoon dried thyme
¼ teaspoon black pepper

1 Heat 1 tablespoon oil in large skillet over medium heat. Add onions; cook 15 minutes or until lightly browned, stirring occasionally.

2 Stir in ¼ teaspoon salt. Add 3 teaspoons vinegar, 1 teaspoon at a time, scraping up browned bits from bottom of skillet.

3 Add mushrooms and ¼ teaspoon salt to skillet; cook 5 minutes or until mushrooms are tender, stirring occasionally. Transfer vegetables to medium bowl; cover to keep warm.

4 Add remaining 1 tablespoon oil to skillet; heat over medium-high heat. Add beef; sprinkle with remaining ¼ teaspoon salt, thyme and pepper. Cook 4 to 6 minutes or until browned, stirring occasionally.

5 Turn off heat; drizzle with remaining 1 teaspoon vinegar. Stir in vegetable mixture.

OLD-FASHIONED MEAT LOAF

[makes 6 servings]

2 teaspoons olive oil
1 cup finely chopped onion
4 cloves garlic, minced
1½ pounds ground beef
1 cup chili sauce, divided

¾ cup old-fashioned oats
1 egg
½ teaspoon salt
½ teaspoon black pepper
1 tablespoon Dijon mustard

1 Preheat oven to 375°F. Heat oil in large skillet over medium heat. Add onion; cook and stir 5 minutes. Add garlic; cook and stir 1 minute. Transfer to large bowl; set aside to cool 5 minutes.

2 Add beef, ½ cup chili sauce, oats, egg, salt and pepper to bowl; mix gently with hands. Pat into 9×5-inch loaf pan.

3 Combine remaining ½ cup chili sauce and mustard in small bowl; spoon evenly over top of meat loaf.

4 Bake 45 to 50 minutes or until cooked through (165°F). Let stand 5 minutes before serving.

TIP When preparing meatloaf, meatballs or burgers, it's important to mix the ingredients gently—overworking the meat mixture can result in a tough and/or dense final dish.

RED WINE OREGANO BEEF KABOBS

[makes 4 servings]

¼ cup dry red wine
¼ cup finely chopped fresh parsley
2 tablespoons Worcestershire sauce
3 cloves garlic, minced
1 tablespoon soy sauce
1 teaspoon dried oregano
½ teaspoon salt

½ teaspoon black pepper
12 ounces boneless beef top sirloin steak, cut into 16 (1-inch) pieces
16 whole mushrooms (about 8 ounces total)
1 medium red onion, cut in eighths and layers separated

1 Combine wine, parsley, Worcestershire sauce, garlic, soy sauce, oregano, salt and pepper in small bowl; mix well.

2 Combine steak, mushrooms and onion in large resealable food storage bag. Add wine mixture; seal bag and turn to coat. Marinate in refrigerator 1 hour, turning frequently.

3 Soak four 12-inch or eight 6-inch bamboo skewers in water for 20 minutes to prevent burning.

4 Preheat broiler. Spray broiler rack with nonstick cooking spray. Alternate beef, mushrooms and two layers of onion on skewers. Arrange skewers on broiler rack; brush with marinade. Discard remaining marinade.

5 Broil 4 to 6 inches from heat source 8 to 10 minutes or until beef is tender, turning occasionally.

TACO-TOPPED POTATOES

[makes 4 servings]

4 Yukon Gold or red potatoes (about 6 ounces each), scrubbed and pierced with fork
½ pound ground beef
½ (1-ounce) package taco seasoning mix
½ cup water

1 cup diced tomatoes
¼ teaspoon salt
2 cups shredded lettuce
½ cup (2 ounces) shredded sharp Cheddar cheese
¼ cup chopped green onions (optional)
Sour cream

1 Microwave potatoes on HIGH 6 to 7 minutes or until fork-tender.

2 Meanwhile, cook beef in large skillet over medium-high heat 6 to 8 minutes or until browned, stirring to break up meat. Drain fat.

3 Stir in taco seasoning mix and water; cook over medium heat 5 minutes, stirring occasionally.

4 Combine tomatoes and salt in medium bowl; stir to blend.

5 Split potatoes almost in half and fluff with fork. Fill with beef mixture, tomatoes, lettuce, cheese and green onions, if desired. Serve with sour cream.

STEAK DIANE WITH CREMINI MUSHROOMS

[makes 2 servings]

2 teaspoons vegetable oil, divided
2 beef tenderloin steaks (about 4
    ounces each), cut ¾ inch thick
¼ teaspoon salt, divided
¼ teaspoon black pepper

⅓ cup sliced shallots or chopped onion
4 ounces cremini mushrooms, sliced
1½ tablespoons Worcestershire sauce
1 tablespoon Dijon mustard

1 Heat 1 teaspoon oil in large skillet over medium-high heat. Add steaks; sprinkle
with ⅛ teaspoon salt and pepper. Cook 3 minutes per side for medium rare or
to desired doneness. Remove to plate; tent with foil to keep warm.

2 Heat remaining 1 teaspoon oil in same skillet over medium heat. Add shallots;
cook and stir 2 minutes. Add mushrooms and remaining ⅛ teaspoon salt; cook
4 minutes, scraping up browned bits from bottom of skillet. Add Worcestershire
sauce and mustard; cook 1 minute, stirring frequently.

3 Return steaks and any accumulated juices to skillet; cook 1 to 2 minutes or until
heated through, turning once.

> **TIP** When a recipe calls for tenting with foil, that means you should cover
> the dish loosely. (Drape a large sheet of foil over the dish and fold it slightly
> in the center like a tent.) This is often done with meat and poultry dishes that
> are browned or grilled and have a crisp crust. Covering the dish tightly would
> cause the food to steam and turn soft, so a loose cover of foil is your best
> tool to maintain heat while keeping the crust intact.

SOUTHWESTERN SLOPPY JOES
[makes 8 servings]

1 pound ground beef
1 cup chopped onion
¼ cup chopped celery
¼ cup water
1 can (10 ounces) diced tomatoes
   with green chiles

1 can (8 ounces) tomato sauce
1 tablespoon packed brown sugar
¾ teaspoon salt
½ teaspoon ground cumin
8 rolls or hamburger buns, split

1 Combine beef, onion, celery and water large skillet; cook over medium-high heat 6 to 8 minutes or until meat is browned, stirring to break up meat. Drain fat.

2 Stir in tomatoes, tomato sauce, brown sugar, salt and cumin; bring to a boil over high heat. Reduce heat to low; cook 20 minutes or until mixture thickens, stirring occasionally.

3 Spoon ⅓ cup meat mixture onto each bun.

> **TIP** You don't have to use beef for Sloppy Joes; you can also make this recipe with ground turkey, chicken, pork or even plant-based crumbles. Whichever you choose, be sure to brown the meat well in the first step to boost the flavor.

ZESTY SKILLET PORK CHOPS

[makes 4 servings]

1 teaspoon chili powder

¾ teaspoon salt, divided

4 boneless pork chops
(4 to 6 ounces each)

2 cups diced tomatoes

1 cup chopped green, red
or yellow bell pepper

¾ cup thinly sliced celery

½ cup chopped onion

1 tablespoon hot pepper sauce

1 teaspoon dried thyme

1 tablespoon vegetable oil

2 tablespoons finely chopped
fresh parsley

1 Rub chili powder and ½ teaspoon salt over one side of pork chops.

2 Combine tomatoes, bell pepper, celery, onion, hot pepper sauce, thyme and remaining ¼ teaspoon salt in medium bowl; mix well.

3 Heat oil in large skillet over medium-high heat. Add pork chops, seasoned side down; cook 1 minute. Turn pork chops; top with tomato mixture. Bring to a boil. Reduce heat to low; cover and simmer 25 minutes or until pork is tender and tomato mixture has thickened.

4 Transfer pork to serving plates with slotted spatula, leaving tomato mixture in skillet. Bring to a boil over high heat; cook 2 minutes or until most of liquid has evaporated. Remove from heat; stir in parsley. Spoon sauce over pork.

CAULIFLOWER, SAUSAGE AND GOUDA SHEET PAN

[makes 6 servings]

1 package (16 ounces) white mushrooms, trimmed and halved

3 tablespoons olive oil, divided

1 teaspoon salt, divided

1 head cauliflower, separated into florets and thinly sliced

¼ teaspoon chipotle chili powder

1 package (about 13 ounces) smoked sausage, cut into ¼-inch slices

2 tablespoons peach or apricot preserves

1 tablespoon Dijon mustard

½ red onion, thinly sliced

6 ounces Gouda cheese, cubed

1 Preheat oven to 400°F.

2 Place mushrooms in medium bowl. Drizzle with 1 tablespoon oil and sprinkle with ½ teaspoon salt; toss to coat. Spread on baking sheet.

3 Combine cauliflower, remaining 2 tablespoons oil, ½ teaspoon salt and chipotle chili powder in same bowl; toss to coat. Spread on baking sheet with mushrooms.

4 Combine sausage, preserves and mustard in same bowl; stir until sausage is well coated. Arrange sausage over vegetables; top with onion.

5 Bake 30 minutes. Remove from oven; place cheese cubes on top of cauliflower. Bake 5 minutes or until cheese is melted and cauliflower is tender.

SIMPLE SLOW COOKER PORK TACOS

[makes 6 servings]

2 pounds boneless pork roast
1 cup salsa
1 can (4 ounces) diced green chiles
½ teaspoon garlic salt
½ teaspoon black pepper
6 (6-inch) corn or flour tortillas, warmed

Lime wedges
Optional toppings: tomatillo salsa, sliced jalapeño peppers, sour cream, shredded cheese and shredded lettuce

SLOW COOKER DIRECTIONS

1 Place pork in slow cooker. Combine salsa, chiles, garlic salt and pepper in small bowl; stir to blend. Pour salsa mixture over pork.

2 Cover; cook on LOW 8 hours.

3 Remove pork to cutting board; let stand 10 minutes. Shred pork into bite-size pieces with two forks.

4 Stir shredded pork into cooking liquid in slow cooker. Serve on warm tortillas with lime wedges and desired toppings.

PEPPERONI PIZZA BAGELS >>

[makes 4 servings]

4 plain or sesame seed bagels
½ cup marinara sauce

1 cup (4 ounces) shredded mozzarella cheese
¼ cup mini pepperoni slices

1 Preheat oven to 400°F. Line baking sheet with parchment paper or foil.

2 Cut bagels in half crosswise with serrated knife. Spread 1 tablespoon marinara sauce over each cut half; top with cheese and pepperoni. Place on prepared baking sheet.

3 Bake 8 to 10 minutes or until cheese is melted and beginning to brown.

PORK TENDERLOIN WITH FIG SAUCE

[makes 4 servings]

1 tablespoon olive oil
1 pork tenderloin (about 1 pound)
1 teaspoon salt
½ teaspoon black pepper

1 jar (about 8 ounces) fig jam or preserves
¼ cup dry red wine

1 Preheat oven to 375°F. Heat oil in large skillet over medium-high heat. Add pork; cook about 3 minutes per side or until browned. Sprinkle with salt and pepper; place in shallow roasting pan.

2 Roast 15 minutes. Meanwhile, combine fig jam and wine in same skillet; cook over low heat 5 minutes or until melted and warm, stirring occasionally and scraping up browned bits from bottom of skillet.

3 Brush small amount of fig sauce over pork; roast 5 minutes or until pork is 145°F. Transfer to cutting board; tent with foil to keep warm. Let stand 10 minutes before slicing. Slice pork; serve with remaining fig sauce.

CHORIZO QUESADILLAS
[makes 6 servings]

1 package (9 ounces) uncooked
    Mexican chorizo sausage,
    casings removed
1 cup coarsely chopped cauliflower
1 small onion, finely chopped
12 (6-inch) flour tortillas

1½ cups (6 ounces) grated chihuahua
    cheese
6 teaspoons vegetable oil
    Salsa, guacamole and sour cream
    (optional)

1 Heat large skillet over medium-high heat. Add chorizo, cauliflower and onion; cook and stir 10 to 12 minutes or until cauliflower is tender. Remove to medium bowl. Wipe out skillet with paper towel.

2 Spread ¼ cup chorizo mixture onto each of six tortillas. Top with ¼ cup cheese and remaining six tortillas.

3 Heat 1 teaspoon oil in same skillet over medium-high heat. Add one quesadilla; cook 2 to 3 minutes per side or until well browned and cheese is melted. Repeat with remaining oil and quesadillas. Cut into wedges; serve with salsa, guacamole and sour cream, if desired.

> **TIPS** To remove sausage from the casing, pinch the sausage in the center and push it outwards in both directions (like squeezing out toothpaste). Or you can use a knife to make a long slit down the center, then peel away and discard the casing.
>
> To keep cooked quesadillas warm, arrange them on a baking sheet and place in a preheated 200°F oven until all the quesadillas are cooked and ready to serve.

RESTAURANT-STYLE BABY BACK RIBS

[makes 4 servings]

1¼ cups water
1 cup white vinegar
⅔ cup packed dark brown sugar
½ cup tomato paste
1 tablespoon yellow mustard
1½ teaspoons salt

1 teaspoon liquid smoke
1 teaspoon onion powder
½ teaspoon garlic powder
½ teaspoon paprika
2 racks pork baby back ribs
(3½ to 4 pounds total)

1 Combine water, vinegar, brown sugar, tomato paste, mustard, salt, liquid smoke, onion powder, garlic powder and paprika in medium saucepan; bring to a boil over medium heat. Reduce heat to medium-low; cook 40 minutes or until sauce thickens, stirring occasionally.

2 Preheat oven to 300°F. Place each rack of ribs on large sheet of heavy-duty foil. Brush some of sauce over ribs, covering completely. Fold down edges of foil tightly to seal and create packet; arrange packets on baking sheet, seam sides up.

3 Bake 2 hours. Preheat broiler. Carefully open packets and drain off excess liquid.

4 Brush ribs with sauce; broil 5 minutes per side or until beginning to char, brushing with sauce once or twice. Serve with remaining sauce.

TIP This recipe shows just how easy it is to make your own barbecue sauce using simple pantry ingredients. You can make it days in advance, store it in the refrigerator and use it for other recipes such as grilled chicken or burgers. But if you'd like to take a shortcut and skip step 1, you can simply substitute your favorite supermarket barbecue sauce and start the recipe with step 2.

MU SHU PORK WRAPS

[makes 4 servings]

1 tablespoon dark sesame oil

1 red bell pepper, cut into short, thin strips

1 pork tenderloin (about 1 pound), cut into strips

1 medium zucchini or yellow squash (or a combination), cut into strips

3 cloves garlic, minced

2 cups prepared coleslaw mix or shredded cabbage

2 tablespoons hoisin sauce

¼ cup plum sauce

4 (8- to 10-inch) flour tortillas or favorite wraps, warmed

1 Heat oil in large skillet over medium-high heat. Add bell pepper; cook and stir 2 minutes. Add pork, zucchini and garlic; cook and stir 4 to 5 minutes or until pork is cooked through and vegetables are crisp-tender.

2 Add coleslaw mix; cook and stir 2 minutes or until wilted. Add hoisin sauce; cook and stir 1 minute.

3 Spread plum sauce down centers of tortillas; top with pork mixture. Roll up to enclose filling; cut diagonally in half.

TIP Asian ingredients like dark sesame oil, hoisin sauce and plum sauce are easy to find in the Asian section of most supermarkets. Store these items in the refrigerator after opening.

CARIBBEAN PORK CHOPS WITH HONEY-GLAZED PEPPERS AND RICE

[makes 4 servings]

2 teaspoons Caribbean jerk seasoning, divided

4 bone-in center-cut pork chops (about 6 ounces each, ½ inch thick)

1 tablespoon vegetable oil

2 bell peppers (red, yellow, green or a combination) cut into thin 2-inch strips

1 tablespoon honey

1 tablespoon balsamic vinegar

1 package (8½ ounces) cooked brown rice

2 teaspoons chopped fresh thyme or parsley

1 Preheat oven to 375°F. Sprinkle 1 teaspoon seasoning over both sides of pork chops.

2 Heat oil in large skillet over medium-high heat. Add pork chops; cook 2 minutes per side or until browned. Transfer pork chops to shallow roasting pan or baking sheet. (Do not wash out skillet.) Bake 6 to 8 minutes or until pork is no longer pink in center.

3 Meanwhile, add bell peppers to same skillet; cook and stir over medium-high heat 3 minutes. Reduce heat to medium. Add honey and vinegar; cook and stir 1 minute. Add rice and remaining 1 teaspoon jerk seasoning; cook and stir 2 minutes or until heated through.

4 Divide rice mixture among four plates; top with pork chops. Sprinkle with thyme; drizzle any juices from roasting pan over pork chops.

BRATWURST SKILLET
[makes 4 servings]

1 pound bratwurst links, cut
    into ½-inch slices
1½ cups sliced onions
1½ cups green bell pepper strips

1½ cups red bell pepper strips
1 teaspoon paprika
1 teaspoon caraway seeds

1 Heat large skillet over medium heat. Add bratwurst; cover and cook about
  5 minutes or until browned and no longer pink in center. Remove bratwurst
  to plate; cover to keep warm.

2 Drain all but 1 tablespoon drippings from skillet. Add onions, bell peppers, paprika
  and caraway seeds; cook and stir about 5 minutes or until vegetables are tender.

3 Return bratwurst to skillet; mix well. Serve immediately.

> **TIP** When you're discarding drippings from a skillet after cooking sausage,
> bacon or other meats, don't pour it down the drain—this can clog up your
> kitchen pipes. You don't want to pour hot fat straight into the garbage
> either, so the best solution is to pour it into a can or heatproof bowl and let
> it cool. (You can refrigerate it to speed up the process.) Once the fat has
> hardened, you can throw it away. Or for bacon grease, store it covered in
> the refrigerator to use for cooking.

GARLIC PORK WITH ROASTED POTATOES
[makes 4 servings]

1 teaspoon garlic powder
½ teaspoon paprika
1 pork tenderloin (about 1 pound)
2 tablespoons olive oil, divided
8 unpeeled new red potatoes (about
   1 pound), scrubbed and quartered

1 teaspoon dried oregano
1 teaspoon salt
½ teaspoon black pepper

1 Preheat oven to 425°F. Spray 13×9-inch baking pan with nonstick cooking spray.

2 Combine garlic powder and paprika in small bowl; sprinkle over all sides of pork.

3 Heat 1 tablespoon oil large skillet over medium-high heat. Add pork; cook about
3 minutes per side or until browned. Place in center of prepared pan.

4 Remove skillet from heat. Add remaining 1 tablespoon oil, potatoes and oregano;
stir to coat, scraping up browned bits from bottom of skillet with spatula. Arrange
potato mixture around pork in prepared pan. Combine salt and pepper in small
bowl; sprinkle over pork and potatoes.

5 Roast about 20 minutes or until pork is 145°F. Remove pork to cutting board;
tent with foil to keep warm. Let stand 10 minutes before slicing.

6 Stir potatoes in baking pan; roast 5 to 10 minutes or until tender and beginning
to brown. Slice pork; serve with potatoes.

PAN-SEARED HALIBUT WITH AVOCADO SALSA

[makes 4 servings]

4 tablespoons chipotle salsa, divided
½ teaspoon salt, divided
4 small (4 to 5 ounces each) or 2 large
(8 to 10 ounces each) halibut
steaks, cut ¾ inch thick
1 tablespoon vegetable oil

½ cup diced tomato
1 ripe avocado, diced
2 tablespoons chopped fresh cilantro
(optional)
Lime wedges

1 Combine 2 tablespoons salsa and ¼ teaspoon salt in small bowl; spread over both sides of halibut.

2 Heat oil in large nonstick skillet over medium heat. Add halibut; cook 4 to 5 minutes per side or until center is opaque.

3 Meanwhile, combine remaining 2 tablespoons salsa, ¼ teaspoon salt, tomato, avocado and cilantro, if desired, in small bowl; mix well. Spoon over halibut; serve with lime wedges.

SEARED SCALLOPS OVER GARLIC-LEMON SPINACH
[makes 4 servings]

1 pound sea scallops (about 12)
¼ teaspoon salt
⅛ teaspoon black pepper
1 tablespoon olive oil
2 cloves garlic, minced

1 shallot, minced
1 package (about 6 ounces) baby spinach
1 tablespoon lemon juice
Lemon wedges (optional)

1 Pat scallops dry with paper towel; sprinkle with salt and pepper.

2 Heat oil in large nonstick skillet over medium-high heat. Add scallops; cook 2 to 3 minutes per side or until golden brown. Remove to plate; tent with foil to keep warm.

3 Add garlic and shallot to skillet; cook and stir 45 seconds or until fragrant. Add spinach; cook 2 minutes or just until spinach begins to wilt, stirring occasionally. Remove from heat; stir in lemon juice.

4 Serve scallops over spinach; garnish with lemon wedges.

TIP It's important to dry off the scallops (and any fish or meat that you are searing in hot oil) in order to get a golden crust. If the seafood or meat is wet when it goes into the pan, it will steam rather than brown.

SOUTHWESTERN TILAPIA WITH RICE AND BEANS

[makes 4 servings]

2 tablespoons all-purpose flour
1 teaspoon salt, divided
¼ teaspoon black pepper
4 tilapia fillets (4 to 6 ounces each), patted dry
2 tablespoons butter, divided
1 can (about 15 ounces) black beans, rinsed and drained

1 can (about 14 ounces) diced tomatoes with chiles
1 package (about 8 ounces) ready-to-serve Spanish rice
¼ teaspoon dried oregano
1 green onion, finely chopped

1 Combine flour, ½ teaspoon salt and pepper in large resealable food storage bag; mix well. Add tilapia; seal bag and shake to coat.

2 Melt 1 tablespoon butter in large nonstick skillet over medium-high heat. Add tilapia; cook 2 minutes per side or until golden brown and fish begins to flake when tested with fork. Remove to plate; tent with foil to keep warm.

3 Melt remaining 1 tablespoon butter in same skillet. Stir in beans, tomatoes, rice, oregano and remaining ½ teaspoon salt. Reduce heat to low; cook 5 minutes, stirring frequently.

4 Arrange tilapia over rice mixture. Sprinkle with green onion.

TUNA STEAKS WITH PINEAPPLE SALSA
[makes 4 servings]

1 medium tomato, chopped
1 can (8 ounces) pineapple chunks
    in juice, drained and chopped
2 tablespoons chopped fresh cilantro
1 jalapeño pepper, seeded and minced
1 tablespoon minced red onion
2 teaspoons lime juice

½ teaspoon grated lime peel
½ teaspoon plus ⅛ teaspoon salt,
    divided
4 tuna steaks (4 to 6 ounces each)
⅛ teaspoon black pepper
1 tablespoon olive oil

1 Combine tomato, pineapple, cilantro, jalapeño, onion, lime juice, lime peel and ⅛ teaspoon salt in medium bowl; mix well.

2 Season tuna with remaining ½ teaspoon salt and black pepper.

3 Heat oil in large nonstick skillet over medium-high heat. Add tuna; cook 2 to 3 minutes per side for medium rare or to desired degree of doneness. Serve with salsa.

TIP Grate the peel of your limes and lemons before you cut them in half to juice them. And if a recipe calls for only the peel, wrap the lime or lemon with plastic wrap and store it in the refrigerator until you need the juice. (Without the skin to protect it, the citrus juice oxidizes and changes flavor; plastic wrap helps to prevent this from happening.)

SHRIMP AND VEGETABLE SKILLET
[makes 4 servings]

¼ cup soy sauce

2 tablespoons lime juice

1 tablespoon sesame oil

1 teaspoon grated fresh ginger

⅛ teaspoon red pepper flakes

2 tablespoons vegetable oil, divided

32 medium raw shrimp (about 8 ounces total), peeled, deveined and patted dry (with tails on)

2 medium zucchini, cut in half lengthwise and thinly sliced

6 green onions, trimmed and halved lengthwise

1 cup grape tomatoes

1 Whisk soy sauce, lime juice, oil, ginger and red pepper flakes in small bowl until well blended.

2 Heat 1 tablespoon oil in large nonstick skillet over medium-high heat. Add shrimp; cook and stir 3 minutes or until shrimp are opaque. Remove to large bowl.

3 Add remaining 1 tablespoon oil and zucchini to skillet; cook and stir 4 to 6 minutes or just until crisp-tender. Add green onions and tomatoes; cook 2 minutes. Add to bowl with shrimp.

4 Add soy sauce mixture to skillet; bring to a boil. Remove from heat. Return shrimp and vegetables to skillet; toss gently to coat.

TIP To devein shrimp, make a shallow cut along the rounded side and use the tip of a paring knife or your fingers to remove the black stringlike vein.

BAJA BURRITOS
[makes 4 servings]

4 tablespoons vegetable oil, divided
3 tablespoons lime juice, divided
2 teaspoons chili powder
1½ teaspoons lemon-pepper seasoning
½ teaspoon salt, divided
1 pound tilapia fillets
3 cups coleslaw mix

½ cup chopped fresh cilantro
¼ teaspoon black pepper
  Guacamole and pico de gallo
  (optional)
4 (7-inch) flour tortillas
  Lime wedges

1 Preheat broiler. Combine 2 tablespoons oil, 1 tablespoon lime juice, chili powder, lemon pepper and ¼ teaspoon salt in large resealable food storage bag. Add tilapia; seal bag and turn to coat. Let stand at room temperature 10 minutes.

2 Spray rack of broiler pan with nonstick cooking spray. Remove tilapia from marinade; discard marinade. Place tilapia on rack.

3 Broil 4 inches from heat source 3 to 5 minutes per side or until center is opaque.

4 Combine coleslaw mix, remaining 2 tablespoons oil, 2 tablespoons lime juice, ¼ teaspoon salt and cilantro in medium bowl; mix well.

5 Layer tilapia, coleslaw mixture, guacamole and pico de gallo, if desired, on tortillas; roll up tightly to enclose filling. Serve with additional pico de gallo and lime wedges.

> **TIP** You can substitute any firm white fish, such as snapper or halibut, for the tilapia.

ROASTED SALMON WITH HORSERADISH SAUCE

[makes 4 servings]

4 salmon fillets (4 to 6 ounces each), patted dry
1 tablespoon olive oil
½ teaspoon salt, divided
½ teaspoon coarsely ground black pepper

½ cup mayonnaise
¼ cup sour cream
2 to 3 teaspoons prepared horseradish
1 teaspoon Dijon mustard
½ teaspoon minced garlic
¼ teaspoon dried rosemary

1 Preheat oven to 400°F. Line baking sheet with heavy-duty foil; spray with nonstick cooking spray.

2 Brush both sides of salmon with oil; sprinkle with ¼ teaspoon salt and pepper, pressing lightly to adhere to fish. Place salmon on prepared baking sheet.

3 Roast 12 minutes or until center is opaque.

4 Meanwhile, combine mayonnaise, sour cream, horseradish, mustard, garlic, rosemary and remaining ¼ teaspoon salt in small bowl; mix well. Serve sauce over salmon.

> **TIP** You can test fish for doneness in several ways. Insert the tines of a fork or a small knife into the thickest part of the fish and peek inside to look at the color—raw fish is shiny and translucent, while cooked fish is opaque. Or gently pull up a piece of the fish with a fork; it will break into flakes easily if it's done. If you encounter some resistance, then it still needs additional cooking time.

SIMPLE SALSA SHRIMP
[makes 4 servings]

1 tablespoon olive oil
¼ cup chopped onion
1 clove garlic, minced
1 cup green salsa
¾ cup dry white wine

1 tablespoon lemon juice
12 ounces medium raw shrimp, peeled and deveined (with tails on)
Hot cooked rice or orzo

1 Heat oil in large skillet over medium-high heat. Add onion; cook and stir 2 minutes or until onion is translucent.

2 Add garlic; cook and stir 1 minute. Add salsa, wine and lemon juice; bring to a boil. Reduce heat to medium-low; simmer 10 minutes.

3 Add shrimp; cook about 2 minutes or until shrimp turn pink and opaque, stirring occasionally. Serve over rice.

> **TIP** Shrimp cook very quickly, so stay close to the stove when cooking them and don't get distracted with other kitchen tasks while the shrimp are in the skillet. The easiest way to check doneness is to look at the color—shrimp start out gray and translucent when raw, then turn pink and opaque when cooked.

TUNA TOMATO CASSEROLE

[makes 8 servings]

2 cans (6 ounces each) tuna in water, drained and flaked

1 cup mayonnaise

1 medium onion, finely chopped

½ teaspoon salt

¼ teaspoon black pepper

1 package (12 ounces) uncooked wide egg noodles

8 to 10 plum tomatoes, cut into ¼-inch-thick slices

1 cup (4 ounces) shredded Cheddar or mozzarella cheese

1 Preheat oven to 375°F. Spray 13×9-inch baking dish with nonstick cooking spray.

2 Combine tuna, mayonnaise, onion, salt and pepper in medium bowl; mix well.

3 Cook noodles according to package directions; drain and return to saucepan. Gently stir in tuna mixture until well blended.

4 Layer half of noodle mixture, half of tomatoes and half of cheese in prepared baking dish; press down lightly. Repeat layers.

5 Bake 20 minutes or until cheese is melted and casserole is heated through.

SPICY CHICKEN RIGATONI

[makes 4 servings]

2 tablespoons olive oil

2 cloves garlic, minced

½ teaspoon red pepper flakes

½ teaspoon black pepper

8 ounces boneless skinless chicken breasts, cut into thin strips

1 cup marinara sauce

¾ cup Alfredo sauce

1 package (16 ounces) mezzo rigatoni or penne pasta, cooked until al dente (see Tip on page 124)

¾ cup frozen peas, thawed

Grated Parmesan cheese (optional)

1 Heat oil in large saucepan over medium-high heat. Add garlic, red pepper flakes and black pepper; cook and stir 1 minute. Add chicken; cook and stir 4 minutes or until cooked through.

2 Add marinara sauce and Alfredo sauce; stir until blended. Reduce heat to medium-low; cook 10 minutes, stirring occasionally.

3 Add pasta and peas; stir gently to coat. Cook 2 minutes or until heated through. Sprinkle with cheese, if desired.

LEMON BROCCOLI PASTA
[makes 2 servings]

1 tablespoon olive oil
2 green onions, sliced
1 clove garlic, minced
2 cups chicken broth
1½ teaspoons grated lemon peel
½ teaspoon salt

⅛ teaspoon black pepper
2 cups fresh or frozen broccoli florets
4 ounces uncooked angel hair pasta
⅓ cup sour cream
2 tablespoons grated Parmesan cheese

1 Heat oil in large saucepan over medium heat. Add green onions and garlic; cook and stir 3 minutes or until green onions are tender.

2 Stir in broth, lemon peel, salt and pepper; bring to a boil over high heat. Stir in broccoli and pasta; return to a boil. Reduce heat to low; cook 6 to 7 minutes or until pasta is tender, stirring frequently.

3 Remove saucepan from heat; stir in sour cream until well blended. Let stand 5 minutes before serving. Sprinkle with cheese.

ONE-POT PASTA

[makes 4 to 6 servings]

8 ounces uncooked rotini pasta

1 can (about 15 ounces) navy
   or cannellini beans

8 ounces grape tomatoes, halved

3 cups packed fresh spinach (about
   3 ounces), stemmed and
   coarsely chopped

6 slices hard salami (2 ounces),
   cut into thin strips

20 pitted Kalamata olives,
   coarsely chopped

⅓ to ½ cup olive oil vinaigrette

3 to 4 tablespoons chopped fresh basil

4 ounces crumbled feta cheese with
   basil and sun-dried tomatoes

1 Cook pasta in large saucepan of boiling salted water according to package
directions until al dente.

2 Meanwhile, drain beans in colander. Drain cooked pasta into beans; shake off
excess liquid.

3 Return pasta with beans to saucepan. Add tomatoes, spinach, salami, olives,
⅓ cup vinaigrette and basil; toss gently to coat. (Heat will wilt spinach slightly.)
Top with cheese; toss again. Add additional vinaigrette if salad seems dry. Cover
and let stand 5 minutes before serving.

TIP Al dente is Italian for "to the tooth," which means there should be some
resistance to the pasta when you bite into it. You want to cook pasta to the
point where it's no longer hard while not allowing it to get too soft or mushy.
To avoid overcooking your pasta, test a piece (by tasting it) at 1 to 2 minutes
less than the directions on the package suggest. (Or some packages now
include an al dente cooking time in their directions.)

SPINACH-CHEESE PASTA CASSEROLE

[makes 6 to 8 servings]

8 ounces uncooked shell pasta

2 eggs

1 cup ricotta cheese

1 package (10 ounces) frozen chopped spinach, thawed and squeezed dry

1 jar (26 ounces) marinara sauce

1 teaspoon salt

1 cup (4 ounces) shredded mozzarella cheese

¼ cup grated Parmesan cheese

1 Preheat oven to 350°F. Spray 1½- to 2-quart baking dish with nonstick cooking spray.

2 Cook pasta according to package directions until al dente; drain.

3 Beat eggs in large bowl with fork. Add ricotta and spinach; stir until well blended. Add pasta, marinara sauce and salt; stir gently to coat pasta.

4 Pour into prepared baking dish; sprinkle with mozzarella and Parmesan. Cover with foil.

5 Bake 30 minutes. Uncover; bake 15 minutes or until casserole is hot and bubbly and cheese is beginning to brown.

GREEK-STYLE TORTELLINI

[makes 4 servings]

1 package (9 ounces) refrigerated
  fresh cheese tortellini
2 tablespoons extra virgin olive oil
1½ teaspoons red wine vinegar
½ teaspoon salt
⅛ teaspoon dried oregano

⅛ teaspoon black pepper
1 can (14 ounces) quartered artichoke
  hearts, drained
1 cup halved grape tomatoes
  or 1 large tomato, chopped
¼ cup finely chopped green onions

1 Cook tortellini according to package directions; drain well. Transfer to large serving
  bowl; let cool 10 minutes.

2 Whisk oil, vinegar, salt, oregano and pepper in small bowl until well blended. Add
  to tortellini with artichokes, tomatoes and green onions; stir gently to coat.

VARIATION For a heartier main dish, add 1 cup diced cooked chicken to
the salad. Increase the oil to 2½ tablespoons and the vinegar to 1 tablespoon.

CREAMY FETTUCCINE WITH PROSCIUTTO AND PEAS

[makes 2 servings]

8 ounces uncooked fettuccine

2 tablespoons olive oil

4 cloves garlic, minced

3 ounces thinly sliced prosciutto or salami, cut into thin strips

1 cup frozen baby peas, thawed

1 cup half-and-half or whipping cream

½ teaspoon salt

½ teaspoon black pepper

1 cup grated Parmesan cheese

Fresh basil leaves (optional)

1 Cook fettuccine according to package directions until al dente; drain.

2 Meanwhile, heat oil in large skillet over medium heat. Add garlic; cook and stir 2 minutes. Add prosciutto and peas; cook and stir 2 minutes. Stir in half-and-half, salt and pepper; cook and stir 3 minutes.

3 Add fettuccine to skillet; stir to coat. Stir in cheese; garnish with basil. Serve immediately.

> **TIP** Prosciutto is a type of dry-cured Italian ham; it can be found at many deli counters and is available presliced with the packaged deli meats.

SPICY ITALIAN SAUSAGE AND PENNE
[makes 4 to 6 servings]

8 ounces uncooked penne pasta
1 pound bulk hot Italian sausage
1 cup chopped sweet onion
2 cloves garlic, minced

2 cans (about 14 ounces each) seasoned diced tomatoes
3 cups broccoli florets
½ cup shredded Asiago or Romano cheese

1 Cook pasta according to package directions until al dente; drain. Return pasta to saucepan; cover to keep warm.

2 Meanwhile, crumble sausage into large skillet. Add onion; cook over medium-high heat 6 minutes or until sausage is no longer pink, stirring to break up meat. Drain fat.

3 Add garlic; cook and stir 1 minute. Stir in tomatoes and broccoli; cover and cook 10 minutes or until broccoli is tender.

4 Add sausage mixture to pasta in saucepan; toss to coat. Sprinkle with cheese.

TIP If hot Italian sausage is not available, you can substitute mild Italian sausage and add ½ teaspoon red pepper flakes to the skillet when cooking the garlic.

CLASSIC MACARONI AND CHEESE
[makes 8 servings]

2 cups uncooked elbow macaroni
¼ cup (½ stick) butter
¼ cup all-purpose flour
2½ cups whole milk

1 teaspoon salt
⅛ teaspoon black pepper
4 cups (16 ounces) shredded Colby-Jack cheese

1 Cook pasta in medium saucepan of salted boiling water according to package directions until al dente; drain and set aside.

2 Melt butter in large saucepan over medium heat. Add flour; whisk until well blended and bubbly. Slowly add milk, salt and pepper, whisking until blended. Cook and stir until milk begins to bubble.

3 Add cheese, 1 cup at a time; cook and stir until cheese is melted and sauce is smooth.

4 Add cooked pasta to saucepan; stir gently until blended. Cook until heated through.

> **TIP** Homemade mac and cheese is suprisingly easy to cook—and once you've tried it, you can make it your own. Add hot pepper sauce or your favorite spice blend for additional flavor, or stir in leftover chicken, chopped cooked bacon or a package of thawed frozen vegetables to make a heartier main dish.

ORZO WITH SPINACH AND RED PEPPER

[makes 4 servings]

4 ounces uncooked orzo pasta

1 tablespoon olive oil

1 medium red bell pepper, diced

3 cloves garlic, minced

¼ teaspoon dried basil

1 package (10 ounces) frozen chopped spinach, thawed and squeezed dry

¼ teaspoon salt

¼ cup grated Parmesan cheese

½ teaspoon lemon-pepper seasoning

1 Prepare orzo according to package directions until al dente; drain.

2 Heat oil in large skillet over medium-high heat. Add bell pepper, garlic and basil; cook and stir 2 to 3 minutes or until bell pepper is crisp-tender. Add orzo, spinach and salt; cook and stir until heated through.

3 Remove from heat; stir in cheese and lemon-pepper seasoning. Serve immediately.

TIP Orzo is a rice-shaped pasta, a versatile variety that's used in soups and salads as well as main dishes. You can also serve it plain as a side dish alongside saucy meat and vegetable dishes. Like other pastas, it should be cooked in a pot of salted boiling water until al dente (usually 8 to 10 minutes). One cup of uncooked orzo will yield about two cups cooked.

SMASHED POTATOES

[makes 4 servings]

4 medium russet potatoes (about
   1½ pounds), peeled and cut
   into ¼-inch cubes
⅓ cup milk
2 tablespoons sour cream
1 tablespoon minced onion

½ teaspoon salt
¼ teaspoon black pepper
⅛ teaspoon garlic powder (optional)
   Chopped fresh chives or French
   fried onions (optional)

1 Bring large saucepan of salted water to a boil over medium-high heat. (Add
about 1 tablespoon salt for every pound of potatoes.) Add potatoes; cook
15 to 20 minutes or until fork-tender. Drain and return to saucepan.

2 Slightly mash potatoes with potato masher. Stir in milk, sour cream, minced
onion, salt, pepper and garlic powder, if desired; mash until desired texture is
reached, leaving potatoes chunky.

3 Cook 5 minutes over low heat or until heated through, stirring occasionally.
Top with chives, if desired.

GARLIC GREEN BEANS AND MUSHROOMS

[makes 4 to 6 servings]

1½ tablespoons olive oil, divided
1 small onion, thinly sliced
8 ounces sliced mushrooms
1 pound fresh green beans, trimmed

1 clove garlic, minced
¾ teaspoon salt, divided
¼ teaspoon black pepper

1 Heat 1 tablespoon oil in large skillet over medium-high heat. Add onion; cook and stir 2 minutes or until beginning to soften. Add mushrooms; cook about 5 minutes or until mushrooms release their liquid and begin to brown, stirring occasionally.

2 Add remaining ½ tablespoon oil, beans, garlic and ½ teaspoon salt to skillet; cook and stir 3 minutes. Reduce heat to medium-low; cover and cook 10 to 12 minutes or until beans are crisp-tender.

3 Season vegetables with remaining ¼ teaspoon salt and pepper; cook and stir 2 minutes.

TIP You can buy mushrooms already sliced or purchase whole mushrooms and slice them yourself. Always clean mushrooms before slicing or chopping, either by rinsing them quickly under cool water or wiping them with a damp paper towel to remove the dirt. Avoid soaking mushrooms in water, which can cause them to become mushy.

BALSAMIC ROASTED VEGETABLES

[makes 4 servings]

2 tablespoons butter, melted

1 tablespoon olive oil

1 tablespoon balsamic vinegar

2 teaspoons honey

1 teaspoon salt

¾ teaspoon dried thyme

¼ teaspoon black pepper

1 large onion, cut into 1½-inch pieces

1 large red or yellow bell pepper (or a combination), cut into 1-inch pieces

6 ounces cremini or white mushrooms, thickly sliced

2 medium carrots, cut diagonally into ¼-inch slices

2 medium zucchini, cut into ½-inch slices

1 Preheat oven to 425°F. Combine butter, oil, vinegar, honey, 1 teaspoon salt, thyme and ¼ teaspoon black pepper in small bowl; mix well.

2 Combine onion, bell pepper, mushrooms, carrots and zucchini on baking sheet. Drizzle butter mixture over vegetables; toss to coat. Spread vegetables in single layer.

3 Roast about 35 minutes or until vegetables are tender and beginning to brown and most liquid has evaporated, stirring halfway through cooking time. Season with additional salt and black pepper, if desired.

CAULIFLOWER BAKE

[makes 4 to 6 servings]

1 medium head cauliflower, broken
   into florets
2 tablespoons butter, melted, divided
½ teaspoon dry mustard
1 teaspoon salt
¼ teaspoon black pepper

⅔ cup whipping cream
1 cup (4 ounces) shredded
   Swiss cheese
½ cup plain dry bread crumbs
1 tablespoon grated Parmesan cheese

1 Preheat oven to 350°F. Spray 2-quart baking dish with nonstick cooking spray.

2 Place cauliflower in prepared baking dish. Combine 1 tablespoon melted butter,
   mustard, salt and pepper in small bowl; mix well. Whisk in cream until well blended.
   Pour mixture over cauliflower.

3 Combine Swiss cheese, bread crumbs, Parmesan and remaining 1 tablespoon
   melted butter in medium bowl; mix well. Sprinkle over cauliflower.

4 Bake 45 minutes or until cauliflower is tender and top is golden brown.

> **TIP** If you're not sure about the size of your baking dish, you can find out by
> filling it with water and then pouring the water into a liquid measuring cup
> to measure the amount. An 8-inch square baking dish holds about 2 quarts;
> a 9-inch square baking dish holds about 2½ quarts; a 13×9-inch baking dish
> holds about 3 quarts.

SAUTÉED SWISS CHARD
[makes 4 servings]

1 large bunch Swiss chard or kale
(about 1 pound)

1 tablespoon olive oil

3 cloves garlic, minced

¾ teaspoon salt

¼ teaspoon black pepper

1 tablespoon balsamic vinegar
(optional)

¼ cup pine nuts or chopped walnuts,
toasted*

*To toast pine nuts, cook in small skillet over medium heat 1 to 2 minutes or until lightly browned, stirring frequently.

1 Rinse chard in cold water; shake off excess water but do not dry. Finely chop stems and coarsely chop leaves.

2 Heat oil in large saucepan over medium heat. Add garlic; cook and stir 2 minutes. Add chard, salt and pepper; cover and cook 2 minutes or until chard begins to wilt. Uncover; cook about 5 minutes or until chard is tender, stirring frequently.

3 Stir in vinegar, if desired. Sprinkle with pine nuts just before serving.

TIP Swiss chard is a leafy green used like spinach and kale in soups, stews, pastas and skillet dishes. To prepare chard for cooking, first tear or cut the leaves from the stalks. The stalks are edible; they just take longer to cook than the leaves so in this recipe they're chopped into very small pieces to even out the cooking times. At grocery stores and farmers' markets you might see chard with different color stalks—white, yellow, red, orange—but they all taste similar and are interchangeable in recipes.

ROASTED CREMINI MUSHROOMS WITH SHALLOTS

[makes 4 servings]

1 pound cremini mushrooms, halved
½ cup sliced shallots
1 tablespoon olive oil
½ teaspoon kosher salt

½ teaspoon dried rosemary
¼ teaspoon black pepper
Fresh rosemary sprigs (optional)

1 Preheat oven to 400°F.

2 Combine mushrooms and shallots on baking sheet. Whisk oil, salt, dried rosemary and pepper in small bowl until well blended.

3 Drizzle oil mixture over vegetables; toss to coat. Arrange in single layer on baking sheet.

4 Roast 15 to 18 minutes or until mushrooms are browned and tender. Garnish with fresh rosemary.

> **TIP** Shallots are a member of the allium (onion) family. They're smaller than onions and more oblong in shape, with a flavor that's milder and sweeter than that of an onion. This subtle flavor makes them especially good to use raw— as in salad dressings—as well as in pan sauces for meat, poutry and seafood.

ORANGE-GLAZED CARROTS

[makes 6 servings]

1 teaspoon salt
1 package (32 ounces) baby carrots
1 tablespoon packed brown sugar
1 tablespoon orange juice

1 tablespoon melted butter
¼ teaspoon ground cinnamon
⅛ teaspoon ground nutmeg
  Grated orange peel (optional)

1 Fill medium saucepan with 1 inch water; stir in 1 teaspoon salt. Bring to a boil over high heat.

2 Add carrots; return to a boil. Reduce heat to low; cover and simmer 10 to 12 minutes or until crisp-tender. Drain well; return carrots to saucepan.

3 Stir in brown sugar, orange juice, butter, cinnamon and nutmeg; cook 3 minutes or until carrots are glazed, stirring occasionally. Taste and season with additional salt, if desired. Garnish with orange peel.

> **TIP** One medium orange will yield about ⅓ cup juice and 1 to 2 tablespoons grated peel. When removing the peel from citrus fruit for cooking (with a grater or citrus zester), use only the outer colored part of the peel, as the white pith underneath has a bitter flavor.

ROASTED RED POTATOES

[makes 4 servings]

2 pounds unpeeled small red potatoes, cut into halves (or quarters if potatoes are larger than 1 inch)
2 tablespoons olive oil

1 teaspoon salt
¾ teaspoon smoked paprika
¼ teaspoon black pepper

1 Preheat oven to 425°F. Spray baking sheet with nonstick cooking spray.

2 Combine potatoes, oil, salt, paprika and pepper in medium bowl; toss to coat. Spread potatoes cut sides down in single layer on prepared baking sheet.

3 Roast 25 minutes or until bottoms are browned. Turn and roast 10 minutes or until potatoes are tender.

TIP When roasting vegetables, it's important to spread them out on the baking sheet and leave a little space between the pieces. This allows air to circulate and promotes browning. If the vegetables are crowded together, they will steam instead of roast and they won't become crisp. If you have more vegetables than can fit on one pan, divide them between two pans.

SWEET POTATO OVEN FRIES

[makes 2 servings]

1 large sweet potato (about 8 ounces)
2 teaspoons olive oil
¼ teaspoon coarse salt

¼ teaspoon black pepper
¼ teaspoon ground red pepper
Honey or maple syrup (optional)

1 Preheat oven to 425°F. Spray baking sheet with nonstick cooking spray.

2 Peel sweet potato; cut lengthwise into long spears. Place in medium bowl. Drizzle with oil and season with salt, black pepper and red pepper; toss to coat.

3 Arrange sweet potato on prepared baking sheet in single layer not touching.

4 Bake 20 to 30 minutes or until lightly browned, turning halfway through baking time. Serve with honey, if desired.

> **TIP** Look for small to medium-sized sweet potatoes that are firm with smooth skin, and avoid those that have darks spots, wrinkles or signs of sprouting. Store them in a cool, dark place (but not in the refrigerator) that allows for air circulation to keep them dry.

CHEESY GARLIC BREAD

[makes 8 to 10 servings]

1 loaf (about 16 ounces) Italian bread
½ cup (1 stick) butter, softened
8 cloves garlic, very thinly sliced

¼ cup grated Parmesan cheese
2 cups (8 ounces) shredded mozzarella cheese

1 Preheat oven to 425°F. Line large baking sheet with foil.

2 Cut bread in half horizontally. Spread cut sides of bread evenly with butter; top with sliced garlic. Sprinkle with Parmesan, then mozzarella. Place on prepared baking sheet.

3 Bake 12 minutes or until cheese is melted and golden brown in spots. Cut bread crosswise into slices. Serve warm.

VARIATION For a spicy garlic bread, sprinkle ¼ to ½ teaspoon red pepper flakes over the garlic. For more Italian flavor, sprinkle ½ teaspoon Italian seasoning over the garlic. Proceed with the recipe as directed.

BLACK BEANS WITH BACON AND POBLANOS

[makes 4 servings]

2 slices bacon
2 medium poblano peppers, chopped (about 1 cup)
1 small onion, chopped
2 cloves garlic, minced

1 teaspoon salt, divided
½ teaspoon chili powder
1 can (about 15 ounces) black beans, rinsed and drained
⅓ cup water

1 Cook bacon in large skillet over medium-high heat about 6 minutes or until crisp, turning occasionally. Drain on paper towel-lined plate. Chop bacon; set aside.

2 Add poblano, onion, garlic, ½ teaspoon salt and chili powder to skillet; cook and stir 5 minutes or until vegetables are crisp-tender. Add beans, water and remaining ½ teaspoon salt; cook 10 minutes or until liquid is absorbed and vegetables are tender, stirring occasionally.

3 Stir bacon into bean mixture just before serving.

> **TIP** Poblano peppers are a mild, dark green Mexican chile pepper. They're about the same size as a bell pepper but are longer and narrower with a pointy tip. They also taste like a bell pepper with a bit of a kick.

SIDES

GREEN CHILE RICE
[makes 4 servings]

1 cup uncooked white rice
2 cups chicken broth
1 can (4 ounces) diced mild
   green chiles
½ medium yellow onion, diced

1 teaspoon dried oregano
½ teaspoon salt
½ teaspoon cumin seeds
3 green onions, thinly sliced
⅓ to ½ cup chopped fresh cilantro

1 Combine rice, broth, chiles, yellow onion, oregano, salt and cumin in large saucepan; bring to a boil over high heat.

2 Reduce heat to low; cover and simmer 18 minutes or until liquid is absorbed and rice is tender.

3 Fluff rice with fork. Stir in green onions and cilantro.

> TIP To chop cilantro, first rinse it well under cool water and blot dry with paper towels or use a salad spinner. Cut off the long stems and chop the leaves with a chef's knife. (The stems are edible but are tougher than the leaves; they are sometimes used in soups, stews and sauces.) If you don't need finely chopped cilantro, you can also cut it with a scissors. Place the leaves in a bowl or measuring cup and use short strokes with a kitchen scissors to cut them into small pieces.

CORNBREAD, APPLE AND SAUSAGE STUFFING

[makes 12 servings]

1 package (16 ounces) bulk
    pork sausage
½ cup (1 stick) butter
1 cup finely chopped onion
1 cup finely chopped celery
3½ cups chopped peeled apples
¾ cup chopped walnuts (optional)

2 teaspoons ground ginger
1 teaspoon salt
½ teaspoon black pepper
1 package (14 ounces) cornbread
    stuffing mix
1½ cups apple cider
1½ cups chicken broth

1 Preheat oven to 325°F. Spray 13×9-inch baking dish with nonstick cooking spray.

2 Brown sausage in large skillet over medium-high heat, stirring to break up meat. Remove to paper towel-lined plate. Drain fat.

3 Melt butter in same skillet over medium heat. Add onions and celery; cook and stir 5 minutes. Add apples; cook 10 minutes, stirring occasionally. Stir in walnuts, if desired, ginger, salt and pepper. Remove from heat.

4 Place cornbread stuffing mix in large bowl; stir in sausage and vegetable mixture. Add cider and broth; stir until well blended. Spoon into prepared baking dish.

5 Bake 25 to 30 minutes or until heated through.

ASPARAGUS RISOTTO
[makes 6 to 8 servings]

5½ cups vegetable broth
⅛ teaspoon salt
4 tablespoons (½ stick) butter, divided
⅓ cup finely chopped onion
2 cups uncooked arborio rice
⅔ cup dry white wine

2½ cups fresh asparagus pieces
   (about 1 inch)
⅔ cup frozen peas
1 cup grated Parmesan cheese
Shaved Parmesan cheese (optional)

1 Bring broth and salt to a boil in medium saucepan over medium-high heat. Keep warm over low heat.

2 Melt 3 tablespoons butter in large saucepan over medium heat. Add onion; cook and stir 2 to 3 minutes or until tender. Add rice; cook 2 minutes or until rice is translucent and coated with butter, stirring frequently. Add wine; cook 3 to 5 minutes or until most of wine is absorbed, stirring occasionally.

3 Add 1½ cups hot broth; cook and stir 6 to 7 minutes or until most of liquid is absorbed. (Mixture should simmer but not boil.) Add 2 cups broth and asparagus; cook and stir 6 to 7 minutes or until most of liquid is absorbed. Add remaining 2 cups broth and peas; cook and stir 5 to 6 minutes or until most of liquid is absorbed and rice mixture is creamy.

4 Remove from heat; stir in remaining 1 tablespoon butter and grated Parmesan. Garnish with shaved Parmesan.

TIP Arborio rice is a variety of short-grain rice from Italy. It's high in the starch called amylopectin; cooking releases this starch which results in a creamier dish with firmer and chewier grains than regular (long-grain) rice.

EASY BBQ BEANS

[makes 6 to 8 servings]

3 thick *or* 5 thin slices bacon, chopped
(½-inch pieces)
1 medium onion, chopped
1 green bell pepper, diced
¼ cup ketchup
2 tablespoons molasses

2 tablespoons packed brown sugar
2 tablespoons coarse-grain or spicy
brown mustard
2 cans (15 ounces each) navy or
Great Northern beans, drained

1 Cook bacon in large saucepan over medium heat 3 minutes, stirring frequently.

2 Add onion; cook 5 minutes, stirring occasionally. Add bell pepper; cook and stir
3 minutes.

3 Stir in ketchup, molasses, brown sugar and mustard; mix well. Stir in beans; cover
and simmer over medium-low heat 20 minutes.

> **TIP** Bacon is easier to chop when it's partially frozen; you can make cleaner
> cuts and it won't slide around under your knife. Just pop it in the freezer for
> 10 to 15 minutes before you're ready to start cooking and the chopping will
> be much easier and neater. (Also be sure your knife is sharp, as a dull knife
> won't work for this task.)

FRUIT AND NUT QUINOA

[makes 6 servings]

1 cup uncooked quinoa
2 cups water
½ teaspoon salt, divided
2 tablespoons finely grated orange peel, plus additional for garnish
¼ cup orange juice
1 tablespoon olive oil

¼ teaspoon ground cinnamon
⅓ cup dried cranberries
⅓ cup toasted pistachio nuts*

To toast pistachios, cook in small skillet over medium heat 1 to 2 minutes or until browned, stirring frequently.

1 Place quinoa in fine-mesh strainer; rinse well under cold running water.

2 Bring 2 cups water to a boil in medium saucepan over high heat; stir in quinoa and ¼ teaspoon salt. Reduce heat to low; cover and simmer 10 to 15 minutes or until quinoa is tender and water is absorbed. Stir in 2 tablespoons orange peel.

3 Whisk orange juice, oil, remaining ¼ teaspoon salt and cinnamon in small bowl until well blended. Pour over quinoa; toss gently to coat. Fold in cranberries and pistachios. Serve warm or at room temperature; garnish with additional orange peel.

TIP Quinoa is rinsed before cooking to remove a natural protective coating called saponin, which can make the grain taste bitter. Packaged quinoa is usually pre-rinsed, but it's a good idea to rinse it again to be sure. Shake off any excess water before using.

SPANISH RICE

[makes 6 to 8 servings]

1 tablespoon olive oil
1 small onion, chopped
2 cloves garlic, minced
2 cups uncooked brown rice,
    rinsed well and drained

1 can (about 14 ounces) diced
    tomatoes with green chiles
3½ cups water
1½ teaspoons salt

1 Heat oil in large saucepan over medium-high heat. Add onion and garlic; cook and stir 2 minutes. Add rice; cook and stir 2 minutes.

2 Stir in tomatoes, water and salt; bring to a boil. Reduce heat to low; cover and simmer 35 to 40 minutes or until rice is tender and water is absorbed. Fluff rice with fork.

> **TIP** Brown rice is a whole grain which contains the bran and the germ; those are the parts of the grain that are removed in the milling process to create white rice. Brown rice is more nutritious than white rice, with a nuttier flavor and denser texture. It also takes about twice as long to cook.

DESSERTS

STRAWBERRY CHEESECAKE PARFAITS

[makes 4 servings]

1½ cups vanilla Greek yogurt
½ cup whipped cream cheese,
    at room temperature
2 tablespoons powdered sugar
1 teaspoon vanilla

2 cups sliced fresh strawberries
2 teaspoons granulated sugar
8 honey graham cracker squares,
    coarsely crumbled (about 2 cups)
Fresh mint leaves (optional)

1 Combine yogurt, cream cheese, powdered sugar and vanilla in medium bowl; beat with whisk until smooth and well blended.

2 Combine strawberries and granulated sugar in small bowl; toss gently to coat.

3 Layer ¼ cup yogurt mixture, ¼ cup strawberries and ¼ cup graham cracker crumbs in each of four parfait glasses or dessert dishes. Repeat layers. Garnish with mint. Serve immediately.

> **TIP** If you love cheesecake, these parfaits offer the same great flavors and textures—crunchy graham crackers, creamy filling and fresh fruit topping—without all the work.

CRUNCHY ICE CREAM PIE

[makes 6 servings]

8 ounces semisweet chocolate, chopped
2 tablespoons butter
1½ cups crisp rice cereal

½ gallon chocolate chip or fudge ripple ice cream, softened
Hot fudge topping

1 Spray 9-inch pie plate with nonstick cooking spray.

2 Combine chocolate and butter in medium saucepan; cook and stir over very low heat until chocolate is melted and mixture is smooth.

3 Remove saucepan from heat. Add cereal; stir until well blended.

4 Spoon mixture into prepared pie plate; press onto bottom and 1 inch up side to form crust. Spread ice cream evenly in crust, mounding slightly in center. Cover and freeze until ready to serve.

5 Let pie stand at room temperature 10 minutes before serving. Drizzle with hot fudge topping.

TIP Use a serrated knife (bread knife) to chop chocolate—the serrated edge grips the chocolate and makes it easier to slice through. It also makes cleaner cuts and causes less of a mess than using a straight-edged knife.

PUMPKIN BREAD PUDDING
[makes 2 servings]

2 slices whole wheat bread
1 cup canned pumpkin
1 egg
2 tablespoons sugar
1 teaspoon vanilla

½ teaspoon ground cinnamon,
   plus additional for garnish
1 tablespoon raisins
Whipped topping (optional)

1 Preheat oven to 375°F. Spray two ovenproof custard cups or ramekins with nonstick cooking spray.

2 Cut bread slices into 1-inch cubes; spread on baking sheet. Bake about 5 minutes or until lightly browned.

3 Combine pumpkin, egg, sugar, vanilla and ½ teaspoon cinnamon in medium bowl; beat with whisk or fork until well blended. Gently stir in toasted bread cubes and raisins. Divide mixture evenly between prepared custard cups.

4 Bake 30 minutes. Serve warm with whipped topping, if desired. Sprinkle with additional cinnamon.

VARIATION If you don't like raisins, you can substitute chocolate chips instead. You can also add 2 tablespoons of chopped nuts for additional flavor and crunch.

SUPER FUDGY BROWNIES

[makes 16 servings]

½ cup all-purpose flour

½ cup unsweetened cocoa powder

½ teaspoon salt

½ cup (1 stick) butter

1 cup sugar

2 eggs

1 teaspoon vanilla

¾ cup semisweet or bittersweet chocolate chips

1 Preheat oven to 350°F. Spray 8-inch square baking pan with nonstick cooking spray. Line with parchment paper, leaving overhang on two sides, and spray again.

2 Sift flour, cocoa and salt into small bowl. Melt butter in medium saucepan over medium heat.* Remove from heat; add sugar and whisk 2 minutes. Add eggs and vanilla; whisk 1 minute or until very well blended.

3 Add flour mixture; stir just until blended. Stir in chocolate chips. Spread batter in prepared pan; smooth top with spatula.

4 Bake 20 to 22 minutes or until edges are set and toothpick inserted into center comes out with moist crumbs. Cool completely in pan on wire rack.

*Or melt butter in medium microwavable bowl; whisk in sugar and proceed with recipe as directed.

WARM MIXED BERRY PIE

[makes 8 servings]

2 packages (12 ounces each) frozen mixed berries

⅓ cup sugar

3 tablespoons cornstarch

2 teaspoons grated orange peel

¼ teaspoon ground ginger

1 refrigerated pie crust (half of 14-ounce package)

1 Preheat oven to 350°F.

2 Combine berries, sugar, cornstarch, orange peel and ginger in large bowl; toss gently to coat. Spread evenly in large (10-inch) ovenproof skillet.

3 Unroll pie crust over fruit mixture; press edge of crust into side of skillet. Cut several slits in crust with small knife to allow steam to escape.

4 Bake 1 hour or until crust is golden brown. Let pie stand 1 hour before serving.

RICH CHOCOLATE PUDDING
[makes 4 servings]

⅔ cup sugar
¼ cup unsweetened cocoa powder
3 tablespoons cornstarch
2 cups milk

1 egg
1 tablespoon butter
½ teaspoon vanilla

1 Combine sugar, cocoa and cornstarch in medium saucepan; mix well. Whisk in milk until well blended; cook over medium-high heat until mixture boils; whisking frequently. Boil 1 minute, whisking constantly.

2 Beat egg in small bowl. Whisk about ½ cup hot milk mixture into egg; whisk egg mixture back into saucepan. Cook over medium heat 2 minutes, whisking constantly.

3 Remove pudding from heat; stir in butter and vanilla until blended. Pour into four individual serving dishes. Serve warm or cover and refrigerate until ready to serve.

RICH MOCHA PUDDING Add 1 to 1½ teaspoons instant coffee granules to sugar mixture in step 1.

SEVEN-LAYER BARS
[makes 2 to 3 dozen bars]

½ cup (1 stick) butter, melted
1 teaspoon vanilla
1 cup graham cracker crumbs
1 cup butterscotch chips
1 cup chocolate chips

1 cup shredded coconut
1 cup chopped nuts
1 can (14 ounces) sweetened
   condensed milk

1 Preheat oven to 350°F.

2 Pour butter into 13×9-inch baking pan; stir in vanilla. Tilt pan to make sure butter entirely covers bottom of pan.

3 Sprinkle graham cracker crumbs over butter. Top with butterscotch chips, chocolate chips, coconut and nuts. Pour condensed milk evenly over nuts.

4 Bake 25 minutes or until lightly browned. Cool completely in pan on wire rack. Cut into bars.

TIP To easily melt butter for this recipe, place the unwrapped stick of butter in the baking pan, then place the pan in the oven while the oven preheats. Remove the pan from the oven as soon as the butter is melted.

BLUEBERRY CINNAMON DUMP CAKE
[makes 12 to 16 servings]

2 packages (12 ounces each) frozen blueberries, thawed and drained or 4½ cups fresh blueberries

⅓ cup sugar

¾ teaspoon ground cinnamon, divided

1 package (about 15 ounces) yellow cake mix

¾ cup (1½ sticks) butter, cut into thin slices

Ice cream (optional)

1 Preheat oven to 350°F. Spray 13×9-inch baking pan with nonstick cooking spray.

2 Spread blueberries in prepared pan. Sprinkle with sugar and ½ teaspoon cinnamon; toss to coat. Top with dry cake mix, spreading evenly. Top with butter in single layer, covering cake mix as much as possible. Sprinkle with remaining ¼ teaspoon cinnamon.

3 Bake 50 to 60 minutes or until toothpick inserted into center of cake comes out clean. Cool at least 15 minutes before serving. Serve with ice cream, if desired.

INDEX

METRIC CONVERSION CHART

VOLUME MEASUREMENTS (dry)

1/8 teaspoon = 0.5 mL
1/4 teaspoon = 1 mL
1/2 teaspoon = 2 mL
3/4 teaspoon = 4 mL
1 teaspoon = 5 mL
1 tablespoon = 15 mL
2 tablespoons = 30 mL
1/4 cup = 60 mL
1/3 cup = 75 mL
1/2 cup = 125 mL
2/3 cup = 150 mL
3/4 cup = 175 mL
1 cup = 250 mL
2 cups = 1 pint = 500 mL
3 cups = 750 mL
4 cups = 1 quart = 1 L

VOLUME MEASUREMENTS (fluid)

1 fluid ounce (2 tablespoons) = 30 mL
4 fluid ounces (1/2 cup) = 125 mL
8 fluid ounces (1 cup) = 250 mL
12 fluid ounces (1 1/2 cups) = 375 mL
16 fluid ounces (2 cups) = 500 mL

WEIGHTS (mass)

1/2 ounce = 15 g
1 ounce = 30 g
3 ounces = 90 g
4 ounces = 120 g
8 ounces = 225 g
10 ounces = 285 g
12 ounces = 360 g
16 ounces = 1 pound = 450 g

DIMENSIONS

1/16 inch = 2 mm
1/8 inch = 3 mm
1/4 inch = 6 mm
1/2 inch = 1.5 cm
3/4 inch = 2 cm
1 inch = 2.5 cm

OVEN TEMPERATURES

250°F = 120°C
275°F = 140°C
300°F = 150°C
325°F = 160°C
350°F = 180°C
375°F = 190°C
400°F = 200°C
425°F = 220°C
450°F = 230°C

BAKING PAN SIZES

Utensil	Size in Inches/Quarts	Metric Volume	Size in Centimeters
Baking or Cake Pan (square or rectangular)	8×8×2	2 L	20×20×5
	9×9×2	2.5 L	23×23×5
	12×8×2	3 L	30×20×5
	13×9×2	3.5 L	33×23×5
Loaf Pan	8×4×3	1.5 L	20×10×7
	9×5×3	2 L	23×13×7
Round Layer Cake Pan	8×1½	1.2 L	20×4
	9×1½	1.5 L	23×4
Pie Plate	8×1¼	750 mL	20×3
	9×1¼	1 L	23×3
Baking Dish or Casserole	1 quart	1 L	—
	1½ quart	1.5 L	—
	2 quart	2 L	—